*Humanism
and
Anti-Humanism*

PROBLEMS OF MODERN EUROPEAN THOUGHT

Series editors
Alan Montefiore
Jonathan Rée

Already published
Consciousness and the Unconscious
David Archard

Humanism and Anti-Humanism
Kate Soper

Philosophy through the Looking-Glass
Language, nonsense, desire
Jean-Jacques Lecercle

Reflexivity
The post-modern predicament
Hilary Lawson

In preparation
Situation
Sonia Kruks

Humanism and Anti-Humanism

KATE SOPER

HUTCHINSON
London   Melbourne   Sydney   Auckland   Johannesburg

Hutchinson and Co. (Publishers) Ltd
An imprint of the Hutchinson Publishing Group
62-65 Chandos Place, London WC2N 4NW

Hutchinson Publishing Group (Australia) Pty Ltd
16-22 Church Street, Hawthorn, Melbourne, Victoria 3122

Hutchinson Group (NZ) Ltd
32-34 View Road, PO Box 40-086, Glenfield, Auckland 10

Hutchinson Group (SA) (Pty) Ltd
PO Box 337, Bergvlei 2012, South Africa

First published 1986

© Kate Soper 1986

Phototypeset in 11 on 12pt Baskerville by
Dobbie Typesetting Service
Plymouth, Devon

Printed and bound in Great Britain by
Anchor Brendon Ltd,
Tiptree, Essex

British Library Cataloguing in Publication Data

Soper, Kate
   Humanism and anti-humanism. – (Problems of
   modern European thought; 4)
   1. Humanism, France
   I. Title   II. Series
   144'.0944   B2424.H8

   ISBN 0 09   162931 4

Contents

Editors' foreword	6
Acknowledgements	7
1 'Blue-nosed misanthropy' and the 'Death of Man': some introductory remarks	9
2 Philosophical anthropology I – Hegel, Feuerbach, Marx	24
3 Philosophical anthropology II – phenomenology and existentialism	54
4 Humanism and political practice	79
5 The death of 'Marxist Man'	96
6 The subjectification of the subject: Lacan and Foucault	120
7 The dancer or the dance? some concluding remarks	146
Index	155

Editors' foreword

During most of the twentieth century, philosophers in the English-speaking world have had only partial and fleeting glimpses of the work of their counterparts in continental Europe. In the main, English-language philosophy has been dominated by the exacting ideals of conceptual analysis and even of formal logic, while 'continental philosophy' has ventured into extensive substantive discussions of literary, historical, psycho-analytic and political themes. With relatively few exceptions, the relations between the two traditions have been largely uncomprehending and hostile.

In recent years, however, continental writers such as Heidegger, Adorno, Sartre, de Beauvoir, Habermas, Foucault, Althusser, Lacan, and Derrida have been widely read in English translation, setting the terms of theoretical debate in such fields as literature, social theory, cultural studies, marxism, and feminism. The suspicions of the analytical philosophers have not, however, been pacified; and the import of such continental philosophy has mostly been isolated from original philosophical work in English.

PROBLEMS OF MODERN EUROPEAN THOUGHT series is intended to help break down this isolation. The books in the series will be original philosophical essays in their own right, from authors familiar with the procedures of analytical philosophy. Each book will present a well-defined range of themes from continental philosophy, and will presuppose little, if any formal philosophical training of its readers.

Alan Montefiore
Jonathan Rée

Acknowledgements

I am deeply grateful to Jonathan Rée and Alan Montefiore, my series editors at Hutchinson, for their unstinting efforts on behalf of this book. I should like to thank them for their astringent and meticulous editing and for their support and encouragement. I should also like to say how much I have appreciated the understanding shown to me by Claire L'Enfant at Hutchinson, and to thank her for her help.

For encouragement, friendship and the right kind of conversations, I should like to thank James Grant, Steve Kupfer, John Mepham, Janet Rée and Erik Svarny.

For much patience and curiosity, I am grateful to my children, Leonie, Jude and Madeleine. Finally, for making life so pleasurable while I wrote the book, and for many painful arguments about its content, my heartfelt thanks to Martin H. Ryle.

Kate Soper
Rodmell

Teleology - developments are due to the purpose which they serve - doctrine of final causes.

1
'Blue-nosed misanthropy' and the 'Death of Man': some introductory remarks

To most people in this country, the term 'humanism' is more or less synonymous with 'atheism'. Even the philosophy student is likely to associate 'humanism' primarily with the secular ethics of the British Humanist Association rather than with any more distinctively philosophical tradition. In the English-speaking world, in fact, 'humanism' has become so closely identified with the promulgation of secularism, that one comes to any work containing the word in its title with the suspicion that it must belong to that rather earnest genre of writing, much of it American, in which 'humanism' is itself presented as a kind of religion – the progressive cult for today's broadminded rationalist. Without calling in question the seriousness of those who engage in this type of writing on 'humanism', it must be said that much of it is written without any sense of the history of the concept, or of its philosophical interest; at its worst, in fact, such writing displays a tendency to speak of 'humanism' as if it were as thing-like in status to the proverbial table, a sort of natural phenomenon, of which anyone handy with their pen could in principle produce a perfect word-copy.

'Humanism', then, is a concept which brings the disjunction between analytical philosophy and continental theory into very sharp relief. For while the term scarcely features in any technical sense in mainstream Anglo-American philosophy, in the vocabulary of continental (and particularly French) theory, it occurs regularly in a usage dating back to the mid nineteenth century, and in recent years has acquired a quite distinctive philosophical content. Opposed, not to theism, but to 'theoretical anti-humanism', it is now very prevalently used, moreover, not to commend but to condemn the school of thinking to which it is applied.

We confront, therefore, a very striking asymmetry not only between the standard usage of the 'humanist' label in this country and its meaning in French philosophy today, but also between the negative charge it has come to acquire in the latter and the almost wholly positive[1]* content it has retained throughout an entire tradition of usage dating back to the Renaissance[2] and still adhered to by those untouched by recent developments in French intellectual life. This is a break upon which it is worth remarking. For despite the very extensive differences of opinion between the self-styled 'humanists' (both past and present) as to what their creed might consist of, none of them has ever been prepared to cede the epithet itself. Indeed 'humanist' doctrine has been so universally regarded as laudable that those who have described themselves as 'humanist' have done so, we must presume, not on account of the definition it lends their thought (a task for which it is, in fact, pre-eminently unsuited) but in order to win approval for it.

Our essential concern here, however, is with an intellectual context that has generated (and latterly come to absorb as part of its common wisdom) remarks of the following order:

Every humanism remains metaphysical. (Martin Heidegger, *Letter on Humanism*)

I believe the ultimate goal of the human sciences to be not to constitute, but to dissolve man. (Claude Lévi-Strauss, *The Savage Mind*)

Making historical analysis the discourse of the continuous and making human consciousness the original subject of all historical development and all action are two sides of the same system of thought. In this system, time is conceived in terms of totalization and revolutions are never more than moments of consciousness. In various forms, this theme has played a constant role since the nineteenth century: to preserve, against all decentrings, the sovereignty of the subject, and the twin figures of anthropology and humanism. (Michel Foucault, *The Archaeology of Knowledge*)

Strictly in respect of theory, therefore, one can and must speak openly of *Marx's theoretical anti-humanism*. (Louis Althusser, *For Marx*)

What is difficult to think today is an end of man which would not be

---

* Superior figures refer to the Notes section at the end of each chapter.

organized by a dialectics of truth and negativity, an end of man which would not be a teleology in the first person plural. The *we*, which articulates natural and philosophical consciousness with each other in the *Phenomenology of Spirit*, assures the proximity to itself of the fixed and central being for which this circular reappropriation is produced. The *we* is the unity of absolute knowledge and anthropology, of God and Man, of onto-theo-teleology and humanism. (Jacques Derrida, *Margins of Philosophy*)

The point of citing these remarks is not to assimilate authors whose concerns and commitments are, in fact, quite disparate, but merely to indicate the gap which separates this discourse from that of humanists in the Anglo-American tradition – for whom it is inconceivable that one might approve of what is 'anti-humanist'. For whom,

What is anti-humanist . . . is familiar in blue-nosed misanthropy, in rude know-nothingness and in all-too-common ignorance and meanness. There is also much anti-humanism in partisan *hubris* and in a general human arrogance or feckless defiance towards the non-human world.[3]

If we 'speak English', then, 'anti-humanism' amounts to a dogmatic rejection of that 'irenic and mediatory ethic[4]' which self-styled humanists have always deemed an essential component of their enlightenment. If we 'speak French', on the other hand, it constitutes itself a new enlightenment from whose purview every form of humanist thinking is revealed as no less obfuscatory and mythological than the theology and superstition which the 'humanist' movement has traditionally congratulated itself upon rejecting.

This brings us to the issue of the technical sense acquired by the terms 'humanism' and 'anti-humanism' in recent French philosophy. For while traditionally 'humanism' is employed approvingly to designate an anthropocentric and secular approach to the study and evaluation of humanity, such anthropocentrism has now itself come under attack from the 'anti-humanists' on the grounds that it mythologizes the object – humankind – of which it aspires to provide a rational or scientific understanding. This theoretical situation can be presented schematically as follows:

Humanism: appeals (positively) to the notion of a core humanity or common essential features in terms of which human beings can be defined

and understood, thus (negatively) to concepts ('alienation', 'inauthenticity', 'reification', etc.) designating, and intended to explain, the perversion or 'loss' of this common being. Humanism takes history to be a product of human thought and action, and thus claims that the categories of 'consciousness', 'agency', 'choice', 'responsibility', 'moral value', etc. are indispensable to its understanding.
Anti-humanism: claims that humanism as outlined above is pre-scientific 'philosophical anthropology'. All humanism is 'ideological'; the ideological status of humanism is to be explained in terms of the systems of thought or 'consciousness' produced in response to particular historical periods. Anthropology, if it is possible at all, is possible only on condition that it rejects the concept of the human subject; 'men' do not make history, nor find their 'truth' or 'purpose' in it; history is a process without a subject.

If the terminology here has a Marxist ring about it, that is because it has been on the basis in particular of Louis Althusser's 'anti-humanist' interpretation of Marx's work, that the theoretical opposition between humanism and anti-humanism has been given most explicit formulation. Yet we are not dealing here with a quarrel internal to Marxism. The 'dissolution' and 'death' of Man, as announced by Lévi-Strauss and Foucault in the 1960s, was to become the dominant theme of the Structuralist movement in the 1970s, and the slogan behind which a relentless and very wide-ranging attack was mounted against the 'humanist' distortions supposedly affecting not only the reading of Marx but practically every field of human study, from psychology to historiography, from literary criticism to anthropology itself. If the dispute over the interpretation of Marx lies at the centre of the humanist/anti-humanist controversy, it by no means exhausts it; and while Althusser may have heralded Marx as the founder of 'theoretical anti-humanism', others among his compatriots have found the primary inspiration for the challenge to humanism not in Marxist 'science', but in Nietzsche's attack upon the Enlightenment ('Death of God') for inaugurating a no less mystifying cult of 'Man'.

In Foucault's words:

In our day, and once again Nietzsche indicated the turning-point from a long way off, it is not so much the absence or the death of God that is affirmed as the end of man (that narrow, imperceptible displacement, that recession in the form of identity, which are the reason why man's finitude has become his end); it becomes apparent, then, that the death of God and the last man are engaged in a contest with more than one round: is it not the last man who announces that he has killed God, thus situating his language, his thought, his laughter in the space of that already dead God, yet positing himself also as he who has killed God and whose existence includes the freedom and the decision of that murder? Thus, the last man is at the same time older and yet younger than the death of God; since he has killed God, it is he himself who must answer for his own finitude; but since it is in the death of God that he speaks, thinks, exists, his murder itself is doomed to die; new goods, the same gods, are already swelling the future ocean.[5]

Nietzsche's assault upon the 'hard atheists' (i.e. the scientists) who are not really atheist at all because they still believe in 'truth' (and hence in 'reason', 'ego', 'spirit', 'motivation', and the many substitutes for God that philosophy inserts into the thinking of European civilization), does more than illuminate the spirit that motivates a good deal of French philosophy today; it also provides us with a bridge back across the Channel to the humanists of the British Humanist Association. For 'hard atheists' they most certainly are, while being at the same time zealous in the pursuit of truth, reason and scientific progress.

Indeed, despite the claim of A. J. Ayer, one of the Association's recent presidents, that the British Humanists are not committed to any set of doctrines and have nothing in common except their atheism,[6] a shared philosophical orientation is clearly detectable: in their concern to avoid the irrationality of religion, they have embraced a positivist conception of the rationality of science. Since they approach human beings as objects of scientific inquiry essentially no different from those found in the non-human world, such humanists assume them to be amenable to very similar forms of investigation. They therefore come to identify a 'scientific' knowledge of humanity with what emerges from studies which attempt to abstract from values and systems of belief. It is a viewpoint well exemplified in an article entitled 'Humanism and Behaviourism' by B. F. Skinner:

What we feel when we have feelings and what we observe through introspection are nothing more than a rather miscellaneous set of collateral products or by-products of the environmental conditions to which behaviour is related. . . . Do I mean to say that Plato never discovered the mind? Or that Acquinas, Descartes, Locke and Kant were preoccupied with incidental, irrelevant by-products of human behaviour? Or that the mental laws of physiological psychologists like Wundt, the stream of consciousness of William James or the mental apparatus of Sigmund Freud have no useful place in our understanding of human behaviour? Yes I do. And I put the matter strongly because if we are to solve the problems that face the world today, <u>this concern for mental life must no longer divert our attention from the environmental conditions of which it is a function.</u>[7]

In somewhat similar vein, H. J. Eysenck, while stressing the importance of 'compassion' in the application of scientific humanism, has insisted that humanism is not a feasible doctrine unless it rests securely on experimental science, particularly behaviourist psychology.[8]

Brisk, businesslike and wholly confident of the powers of science to solve the problems besetting humanity, this is a mode of humanism that approaches human affairs on the model of the industrial enterprise, where all can be set to rights provided we adopt the more efficient management techniques afforded by scientific and technological development. Enlightenment rationality can thus be interpreted in a manner that legitimates the continual surbordination of natural resources and human talents to values of growth and economic prosperity; happiness is to be achieved not through any alteration of values or of the 'needs' they breed and endorse, but by organizing the environment in such a way that it corresponds more closely to the demands that our behaviour reveals we possess.

This 'technical fix' humanism has little in common with the portrayal by the Renaissance humanists of man as a 'free and sovereign artificer' determining his 'own nature without constraint from any barrier';[9] nor should we suppose that the eighteenth-century 'Enlightenment' humanists would have found their wisdom confirmed in the manner in which the industrialized nations of the globe have today 'consolidated' their control over nature by the most irresponsible plundering of its resources. Yet a profound confidence in our powers to come to know and thereby to control our environment and destiny lies at the heart of every humanism; in this sense, we must acknowledge a continuity of theme, however warped it may have become with the passage of time, between the Renaissance celebration of the freedom of humanity from any transcendental hierarchy or cosmic order, the Enlightenment faith in reason and its powers, and the 'social engineering' advocated by our contemporary 'scientific' humanists.

We can trace a similar continuity of theme in the anti-theological component of humanist thought. For while Renaissance humanism by no means implied any overt attack on religion of the kind we associate with the period of the Enlightenment, the anti-clericalism of the latter has its roots in the resistance to medieval church dogma that was characteristic of the Italian movement; and the hardening of this resistance into a committed atheism goes along with a progressive confirmation of humanity's powers of self-determination in the development of science and its successful application. Disenchantment with a 'magical' universe of nature and the abandonment of religious or mythological accounts of its mysteries comes to be seen, therefore, as an essential condition of our release from thraldom to its necessities; while Francis Bacon's assumption that it is only 'vain notions and blind experiments' that forbid a 'happy match between the mind of man and the nature of things',[10] was to find repeated justification in the astonishing capacity of *homo sapiens* to harness nature in the service of its own ends – a capacity which appeared increasingly to distance it from any other species inhabiting the planet – and to bear daily witness to the truth that 'man' is indeed the 'measure of all things'.

In this sketch of humanist thought, the positivistic humanism of the British Humanist Association has been presented as a direct heir of the Enlightenment; conversely, therefore, we shall be led to think of the contemporary anti-humanist movement in France as a neo-Nietzschean attack upon the Enlightenment commitment to truth, reason and scientific progress. To portray the matter in this way would none the less be vastly over-simple; and for two main reasons.

First, we must recognize the extent to which the conception of the Enlightenment is itself profoundly and permanently riven by the experience of the industrial revolution. Capitalist industrialization, by provoking the question of the 'humanity' of science and technology, put an end to an unquestioned faith in the harmonization of human progress with the dictates of nature, and thus brought about a polarization between the enthusiasts of science and technical progress and the advocates of the human and natural values supposedly endangered by industrial development. Cataclysmic in its effects on the natural environment and radically disruptive of any belief in the inevitable congruence of human happiness with the march of science, the industrial revolution was to push apart elements of thinking that had been previously maintained, albeit precariously, in more integral form. The cleavage was thus established in the nineteenth century between those who revelled in the heady testimony of capitalist industry to secure our mastery over nature, a process they associated with a triumph of reason over 'animal' instinct and reactionary superstitions, and those who reacted by stressing our organic relations with the rest of nature.[11] For this latter 'romantic' vein of humanist thought, more ecologically aware and often nostalgic in its yearnings for the pre-industrial age, it was not Man's place 'outside and against' nature that was emphasized, but his very special situation within it.

There are certainly elements of this romantic humanism that pre-date the industrial revolution. For example, the resistance to mechanistic conceptions of human nature and the stress on the emotional qualities which distinguish us from the rest of the natural world are characteristic of Renaissance humanism and traceable in Epicureanism. However, it is first and foremost inspired by antagonism to the ruinous effects of industrialization and characterized by intellectual opposition to the 'justifying logics' of utilitarianism and positivism to which that gave rise.[12]

This brings us to a major qualification that must be made of the suggestion that theoretical anti-humanism has as its main target the faith in scientific progress associated with Enlightenment 'humanism', for the humanist tradition that has recently come under attack from French structuralism and post-structuralism is itself anti-scientific in its general orientation. It is the 'humanism' of the phenomenologists and existentialists, whose own critique of modern industrial society places it at the opposite pole from the positivism of post-war British humanism.

Indeed, it was in the name of 'science' that the structuralist movement first launched its attack on humanist 'mythology'. Inspired initially by Ferdinand de Saussure's success in founding a 'science' of linguistics based on exclusive study of the governing system of language (*langue*) as opposed to its manifestation in particular languages (*langages*), the structuralists contrasted the objectivity and scientificity of the study of structures underlying social and cultural phenomena to the subjectivism of a 'humanist' emphasis on creativity, freedom and purpose. They argued that since conscious experience is itself only explicable in terms of the unconscious and unwilled systems that govern its production, any attempt to account for it at the level of consciousness itself must result in an evolutionary and ethnocentric perspective that is profoundly unscientific: the 'humanist' interpretation views the past as *developing towards* the present whose 'consciousness' is projected back upon it; it views the 'primitive' from the standpoint of its own 'civilization', and so on.

It is true that the original structuralist commitment to scientific objectivity has ceded in the 'post-structuralism' of Foucault and Derrida to a Nietzschean denunciation of the quest for 'truth' as itself a humanist folly. For paradoxical as it may seem, the rejection of the possibility of truth has followed as a logical sequel to the veritable obsession with language as the key to the understanding of all aspects of individual and social being. Derrida has argued, for example, that if it is the case, as Saussure rightly maintained it was, that the signs of language are significant only by virtue of their relations with all the other signs of the system, then strictly speaking meaning always inheres in the play of differences, and is never truly 'present'. The world itself is text, and there can be no reference to a pure meaning prior to language and 'expressed' in it. In recognizing the 'subordination' of language to what it signifies, Saussure's account of language therefore embodies – necessarily yet falsely – a 'logocentric' appeal to that which is 'immediately present to thought'. The fundamental 'error' here, says Derrida (and his argument bears direct comparison to that of Wittgenstein), lies in thinking of meaning as modelled on an immediate self-evidence to the speaker. He associates it with the 'falsity' of treating writing as representative of speech, and, more broadly, with the 'falsity' of philosophy's orientation towards an original and ever present truth or certainty.

The 'post-structuralist' quarrel with structuralism does not in any sense, therefore, involve a return to 'humanist' premises. On the contrary, it challenges the residual 'humanist' invocation of 'presence' upon which structuralist argument relies, and its attack upon science is itself conducted from an 'anti-humanist' perspective. Indeed, post-structuralism is if anything, even less tolerant than structuralism of any explanation that refers us to the experience of the human subject as if to a point of 'origin'.

From a Nietzschean, 'post-structuralist' point of view the self-styled 'humanists' of the British Humanist Association are, indeed, 'humanist' – because they remain committed to the idea of 'science' and the progress it permits. But they espouse much, of course, that is *theoretically* anti-humanist – and in that sense they can be aligned with the structuralist and post-structuralist movement. By whatever other gulfs of philosophy, style and politics they may be divided, both families of thinkers would agree that there is no viable view of the subject as a locus of beliefs, values and intentions. In this sense, an antithetical terminology conceals beneath it a certain measure of methodological agreement.

Any such comparisons between these very different traditions, however, are further complicated by political considerations. For while Anglo-American 'scientific' humanism has methodological features in common with structuralist anti-humanism, its overall political allegiance is to those liberal bourgeois values that the 'humanist' Jean-Paul Sartre found so odious – to the extent that he toyed at one point with the idea of describing his own political standpoint as 'anti-humanist'.[13] We must avoid the mistake, that is, of directly identifying the 'humanism' which is the target of the anti-humanist polemic in France with the humanism of liberal theory, based as that is on metaphysical assumptions which phenomenology and existentialist theory quite explicitly reject. Inspired by Hegel, Husserl and Heidegger – to whose work they bring an 'anthropologizing' reading[14] – the French humanists have wanted to distinguish their own theory from any philosophy rooted in the idea of a universal, predetermining 'human nature' or 'essence' of humanity. It is, indeed, a defining quality of their 'humanism' that it recognizes the historicity of human culture and the problems which it poses for any universalizing discourse about the 'human condition'. Emphasizing the situatedness of the individual within society, it rejects the 'isolated' individual invoked by liberal theory together with the contrast between the 'social' and the 'individual' which such a viewpoint imposes. At the same time, however, it insists that individuals are autonomous within society in the sense that is is their actions which lie at the source of what is social. It is human beings who create the structures and institutions of society; they who are constitutive of social life; and they who are able, therefore, in the last analysis, to control its progress. The 'structures of relations' that, according to the anti-humanist argument, must be viewed as constitutive of human subjectivity, are themselves, according to the humanists, accountable ultimately to the constituting activity of those subjects.

While the thrust of the humanist thought with which we are here primarily concerned is thus opposed to the abstraction characteristic of liberal humanist theory, it still refuses to allow that any exhaustive analysis of what is historically specific – whether it is individuals or their objective circumstances of existence – can be given in terms of the determination of 'subjectless' structures and relations: the distinctive role of human activity in the creation of historical conditions of existence remains, in this humanist conception, irreducible.

In taking this view the humanists argue that the causality brought into play by collective human action differs in kind from that which operates in the non-human, 'natural' world. No matter how 'irrational' and unwilled the consequences of concerted human activity, the activity itself, by virtue of its conscious and intentional character, produces effects that differ in kind from those of any non-rational or mechanical agency. Their claim is not simply that one cannot hope to offer any adequate interpretation of human historical activity that abstracts from the meanings, values and intentions that individuals bring to that action. The point is rather that history differs from natural process in its very nature, in having as its subject matter the creations of moral and rational agents. For the humanist, meaning is literally part of the being of history, because history is itself contrived by those who act in the light of reasons, values and beliefs.

If we observe natural process the question of valued significance does not even arise; if we observe history, it arises compulsively, not only because of its subject-matter (valuing and conscious beings) but also because the observer is by his own moral and intellectual nature a creature of these compulsions. To deny significance to history is not to adopt a 'neutral' or scientific, extra-historical posture: it is to make a particular kind of declaration of value.[15]

According to the humanist, history derives its particular 'non-natural' status from the fact that it is the product of a form of activity (human activity) which differs in kind from the behaviour of other species. It is in the light of this argument that we should understand the particular preoccupations of the recent debate between 'humanists' and 'anti-humanists'. For while a more traditionally 'humanist' concern with the relations of humanity to nature underlies the controversy and is throughout implicit to it (together with ontological questions concerning the 'being' of humanity and its continuity or difference from natural 'being'), the most explicit concern has been with the status of history itself, and with the question of who – if anyone – 'makes' it.

It is a controversy, we might add, in which the positions of both parties have been frequently misrepresented, even directly falsified. One reason for this is the inherent ambiguity in the humanist claim that 'men make history'. For there is clearly more than one interpretation of this slogan. We may take it to mean little more than that history is the aggregate of human acts. What is emphasized by such an interpretation is the non-natural or human quality of history rather than the role of individual or collective deliberation in bringing about historical outcomes. One recognizes, that is, that it is the intentional projects and consciously undertaken activities of human individuals that serve 'to make history' without necessarily being committed to the view that there is a trans-individual meaning or purpose directing those activities or being brought to realization through them.

But there is another interpretation of 'men make history' often imputed to the humanists and quite frequently endorsed by them. This is the claim that everything which is 'historical' is intentionally brought about by human agents in an attempt to control collective existence. A good deal of non-Marxist historiography adopts this outlook when it views history in terms of the intentions of statesmen, the acts or omissions of generals, the plans of this or that faction, and so forth. Yet there is also a continual slippage in the Marxist humanist position between the claim that social process is an irreducibly *human* process and the idea that 'history' is the working out of an essentially human purpose whose final act will be consummated through the conscious seizure of control by a particular social grouping. Indeed, as we shall see, Marxist 'humanism' is itself ambivalent, at times suggesting that 'de-alienation' is the realization of a *potentia* immanent in humanity since its origin, and of which the proletariat is the 'world-historical' vehicle, and at other times confining its argument to more modest claims about the role of human agency in the creation of historical process.

The two interpretations are themselves linked in so far as the more restricted argument implies that control can and should be asserted to offset the 'irrational' and *unintended* consequences of a dispersed mass of private *intentional* acts; and it is, of course, only with the advent of Marxist theory that the project of controlling or 'making' history in this latter sense has been put on the political agenda. The 'humanist' theory that directs attention to the 'unwilled' products of concerted human action is also the humanist theory that aspires to a conscious project of total human emancipation through social revolution.

In projecting a future in which human beings would seize control of the social process and convert it to their own ends, Marx placed great weight upon the liberating effects of a scientific understanding of that process; at the same time, of course, he singled out the proletariat as the bearer of 'universal' emancipation and at times presented it as the agent of realization of an abstract human essence. We shall discuss these ambiguities in due course. Here let it simply be said that while we may allow that concerted deliberate action by a class or political grouping to assert control over social process is a form of 'making history' in the strong sense (i.e. it represents a deliberate attempt to intervene to shape collective destiny), we may not want to accept that such action in any sense represents a stage in the fulfilment of a world-historical mission. We need to distinguish, therefore, between two levels of humanist argument – between the assertion of the constitutive role of individuals in the making of history, and the assertion that history itself is the working-out of an immanent human purpose. One can be humanist in the first sense without being committed to a teleological view of history or to the idea that there is a particular social grouping 'destined' to realize humanity's essential 'being' or historic purpose.

Anti-humanist argument, as we shall see, has tended to conflate these two positions and to assume that both are present in any humanist argument. But it is perfectly possible to accept that historical significance is not to be explained in terms of the actualization of an immanent essence or 'world-spirit', without being committed to the view that humanist categories must be dispensed with altogether and history itself conceived as natural process bereft of any intrinsic intelligibility.

Notes

1 A notable exception is T. E. Hulme, who in his *Speculations: Essays on humanism and the philosophy of art*, ed. H. Read (London 1954), employed the term 'anti-humanism' to mark his dissent from Rousseauan ideas of the infinite perfectability of humankind. See also R. Williams, *Culture and Society* (Harmondsworth 1961), pp. 191–5.
2 We might note, however, that it was primarily as teachers or students of Classical learning engaged in a *renascentia romanitatis* – a return to ancient civilization in which the 'humanity' of Classical Studies was

set against the supposed 'barbarism' (Latin contrasts the '*barbarus*' – the foreign, or different-sounding – to the '*humanus*' as the known and cultivated) of medieval scholasticism and its perversions of the teachings of Plato and Aristotle – that the Italians of the fourteenth and fifteenth centuries were referred to as '*umanisti*'. The key term, in fact, was '*studia humanitatis*', and the evidence suggests that the Italian word '*umanista*' was not in use before the end of the fifteenth century (the earliest dated instance is in 1512). '*Umanismo*' is an even later coinage. The more literary-philosophical sense of the term 'humanism' only becomes fully established in the late nineteenth century. See Augusto Campana, 'The Origin of the Word "Humanist"', *Journal of the Warburg and Courtauld Institutes*, **IX** (1946), pp. 60–73.

3 Paul Kurtz (ed.), *The Humanist Alternative* (London 1973), p. 42.
4 ibid., p. 65.
5 ibid., p. 385.
6 A. J. Ayer (ed.), *The Humanist Outlook* (London 1968), p. 3.
7 ibid., p. 101.
8 ibid., p. 265.
9 The words are those which Pico della Mirandola (1463–94) attributes to God in his *Oration on the Dignity of Man*:

> I have given you, Adam, neither a predetermined place nor a particular aspect nor any special prerogatives in order that you may take and possess these through your own decision and choice. The limitations on the nature of other creatures are contained within my prescribed laws. You shall determine your own nature without constraint from any barrier, by means of the freedom to whose power I have entrusted you. I have placed you at the centre of the world so that you might see better what is in the world. I have made you neither heavenly nor earthly, neither mortal nor immortal so that, like a free and sovereign artificer, you might mould and fashion yourself unto that form you yourself shall have chosen.

The vision projected in the *Oration* of a 'peaceful co-existence' between philosophies, underlies the arguments for religious tolerance that figure so centrally in the 'humanism' advocated later by Erasmus (1466–1535) and Thomas More (1478–1516).

10 See Theodor Adorno and Max Horkheimer, *Dialectic of Enlightenment* (London 1979; first published New York 1944), especially the essay entitled 'The Concept of Enlightenment', where the establishment

of Enlightenment abstraction and utilitarianism is associated with the extirpation of animism and of the 'specific representations' of magical and mythological attitudes to nature.

11 See Gareth Stedman Jones's portrayal of what he terms the 'nature/science-industry' couple in 'The Marxism of the Early Lukács', *Western Marxism* (London 1977), pp. 18–22.

12 As exemplified in Romantic poetry of the nineteenth century. In opposition to the 'Romantic' stress on the vast potential for fulfilment that resides in each of us, and on the freedom and intrinsic powers of the individual, a more utilitarian current of humanist thought seized on the opportunities for *moulding* the individual that seemed revealed by the new rationality: if human beings were not made in Heaven, then they could be produced on Earth, through the right education and proper adjustment of circumstance. This *'tabula rasa'* conception is fundamental to Robert Owen's 'environmentalist' theory of human improvement. It also finds expression in the 'philanthropy' of various educative schemes and 'Systems' of the kind parodied by Dickens in *Hard Times* and Meredith in *The Ordeal of Richard Feverel* (where Sir Austin Feverel is described as 'one in whom parental duty, based on the science of life, was paramount: a Scientific Humanist, in short').

13 Thus Roquentin in *Nausea* (with whom Sartre has admitted his identification) in the course of his dialogue with the Autodidact vilifies everything 'humanist', and elsewhere expostulates: 'I don't want to be integrated, I don't want my good red blood to go and fatten this lymphatic beast: I will not be fool enough to call myself "anti-humanist" I *am not* a humanist, that's all there is to it.' (New York 1959), p. 160.

14 For a discussion of this, see Jacques Derrida, 'The Ends of Man', in *Margins of Philosophy* (first published in France 1972), p. 111f. While criticizing the anthropocentric metaphysics that govern the philosophy of Hegel, Husserl and Heidegger, Derrida argues that they have been given an overly 'humanist' reading by the existentialists and phenomenologists (and for that reason also have been too readily dismissed by the 'anti-humanists'). See esp. pp. 118–19.

15 E. P. Thompson, *The Poverty of Theory, and other essays* (London 1978), p. 137.

2
Philosophical anthropology I – Hegel, Feuerbach, Marx

Humanist thought is very commonly described as 'anthropocentric': it places 'Man' at the centre. But there are different ways of doing so. One is to assume from the outset an opposition between an 'external', objectively existing world on the one hand, and human subjects possessed of consciousness on the other. In this view, 'Man' is conceived as standing 'outside' the reality that is given to him in consciousness. It is a standpoint that promotes and endorses an instrumental conception of the relations between humanity and the non-human or 'natural' world: Nature exists for Man, who by means of an objective knowledge of its workings, harnesses it in the service of human ends.

What we might term an 'idealist' humanism, on the other hand, argues that the world exists only in so far as it is reflected upon and understood in thought, and that since thought is an exclusively human property, the world exists only by virtue of its conceptualization by 'Man'. Such 'idealist anthropocentricity' can be given both more and less solipsistic formulations. Those who claim that the world is constituted in thought will need to make clear whether they attribute its existence to the thought of particular individuals, or to a collective or 'transcendent' mind of which the actual minds of men and women are merely vehicles or instantiations. On the whole, those who have argued for an idealist view (Kant in a partial sense, Fichte, Schelling and Hegel more thoroughly) have understood the matter in this latter sense. Since they regard individual minds as subordinate to a transcendent consciousness, it is perhaps inappropriate to speak of their thought as 'anthropocentric'. None the less their concern throughout is with the 'truth' or 'end' of Man: it is human purpose and self-realization that is fulfilled in the realization of the Absolute Idea.

A third form of anthropocentricism (which some would attribute to Hegel), is what we might term 'dialectical'. According to this conception, the relationship of 'humanity' to 'nature' is to be understood as a totality: the world is what it is as a result of its being lived in and transformed by humanity, while humanity in turn acquires its character through its existence and situation in the world. Thought, therefore, is concerned with a world as lived through a subject, and of which that subject is thought to be a part. While granting independent existence to the world, such a position also wants to stress the active and creative role of human subjects in its making. This creativity can be understood primarily in terms of the transformative powers of human production and labour, or primarily in terms of the meaning (and hence Being – since meaning is conceived as part of Being) that human beings bring to their world and reveal it to contain.

Since, according to this viewpoint, the totality of subject–object (humanity–world) is a historical product, knowledge of it must likewise be historical and relative. If consciousness is in the world, and the relationship is dialectical between that which thinks and that which is thought, then there is no transcendent place from which a 'pure' thought can contemplate the world and its own relation to it. Against the suggestion, therefore, that any humanist thought must rest on an essentialist appeal to an abstract, ahistoric 'being' of humanity, it would seem that dialectical thought is committed to anti-essentialism. Yet a concern for the 'truly human' is common to dialectical thinkers whether expressed in terms of 'realization of species-being' (Marx), or as the achievement of a rationality that could understand the world in its 'total and universal truth' (Husserl), or as an authentic 'living for death' (Heidegger), or as the responsibility that derives from total human freedom (Sartre). And this is certainly a modality of thinking difficult to reconcile with a strict commitment to anti-essentialism and historical relativism.

We might note, furthermore, the liability of dialectical anthropocentrism to be pulled towards one or other pole of the opposition it is attempting to sustain. It yields to idealism when, under the influence of its insistence that thought is as real as that which it thinks about, it comes to treat all reality as thought reality; on the other hand, when the reality of the non-thought, of that which exists independently of its concept, is stressed, then it risks falling back into a denial of the reality of consciousness: thought and meaning are no longer conceived as part of the being, but as external to it and merely 'reflective' of it.

It is against this tension or elasticity in dialectical thinking, and its tendency to recoil to one or other of the poles of being and consciousness which it attempts to synthesize, that the humanist currents with which we are here concerned develop and acquire their particular character. It is crucial to the understanding of these that we place them in the context of Hegel's dialectical response to Kant, and the opposing 'idealist' and 'realist' interpretations that have been placed upon it.

From transcendental to absolute idealism

While Hume had argued that we had no basis for belief in the existence of any necessary order or rationality guiding Nature and ensuring our harmonization with it, Kant attempted to transcend the crisis precipitated by scepticism by theorizing the necessity of a conflict between reason and nature. While crediting the intellect with powers of ordering the universe, he insisted that, so far as human beings are concerned, all such capacities are subject to the constraints of experience. We actively organize a world to whose deliverances we also stand in a relation of passive receptivity. What is known is therefore entirely a function of *a priori* forms of receptive sensibility and categories of active understanding; we can know nothing of reality as it is in itself. Though we are bound to strive after Absolute Knowledge, and the freedom from the incompleteness and contingency of experience that goes with it, our thought will always in fact be subject to perception. We aim to attain to a realm of freedom where we are no longer in thrall to nature, and by following the command of duty we must hope to attain to perfect happiness; but the limits of our understanding are such that we can provide no final guarantees that freedom is attainable or virtue rewarded.

Fichte, Schelling and Hegel form a trio of post-Kantian philosophers convinced that Kant was essentially right in his view that nature as we know it has no existence independent of the human mind. But they rejected his phenomenal/noumenal distinction. Sharing Kant's conception of Nature as posing a challenge to which humanity could only rise in the development of its essential 'spirituality' or 'moral being' they reject the suggestion that there is an inevitable constraint from the side of the 'object' upon the thought of the 'subject'. Hence, for example, Fichte's anti-Kantian insistence upon the complete and total independence of man, whom, he claims, 'exists absolutely in and through himself'.[1] Fichte argues that Kant was wrong to attribute the cause of our thought to a noumenal realm; consciousness – or ego – is itself founding and constitutive, and there is no reason in principle why human freedom should be limited by the 'pull' of nature and object-bound forms of existence and determination.

Having refused to attribute the phenomena of consciousness to any world 'outside', Fichte had no alternative but to argue that both the form and content of experience were the product of the activity of mind. But if this 'mental' source of experience was to account for, first, the similarity between experiences and second, the seemingly obvious truth that things continue to exist whether or not individuals do so, then it clearly could not be identified with any individual mind. The Fichtean 'transcendental ego' is therefore an absolute, trans-historical and trans-individual consciousness of which empirical egos are the finite instantiations. The occurrence of phenomena for this transcendental ego is explained – in terms of its positing of a non-ego, or objective counterpart of itself in the world, wherein it is able to reflect upon itself and arrive at self-knowledge.

According to Fichte, therefore, the world as we ordinarily know it provides the vehicle for humanity's moral pursuit of absolute self-realization: our ultimate and final duty is towards the actualization of our essential freedom, a goal that Fichte regards as attainable only through a continuous practical struggle against the temptation to view ourselves as unfree – as determined by natural law and dependent for our consciousness upon it. To the extent that history is itself continuous, however, our voyage in moral transcendence must itself be endless. We are forever *en route* to a goal that is infinitely deferred. It is part of Hegel's attack on both Kant and Fichte that they view the reconciliation of subject and object, essence and existence, as a merely regulative ideal rather than an attainable state of affairs.

Fichte has also been criticized for the manner in which he made use of his philosophy of freedom to argue the desirability of measures, such as compulsory State education, designed to propel the ego along the path to self-realization and absolute freedom. There is no doubt that Fichte (in effect following Rousseau), nourished conceptions about 'forcing people to be free' and about the essential identity of the interests of the individual with those of humanity as a whole, which would now be regarded with misgivings. Nevertheless, we must also recognize Fichte's originality in founding a dialectic that made no appeal to any extra- or supra-human principle of organization and development: human history, as he conceived it, is not God's work but the self-creation of a species purposefully bent on the attainment of an absolute knowledge of its own development.

Since, however, the subject of this humanist dialectic is the transcendental ego conceptualized as the universalization of individual wills, Fichte inevitably plays down the importance of individual uniqueness and self-expression to the realization of a genuinely emancipated human society. In this sense, the richness and multiplicity of actual 'finite' life comes to be viewed as merely contingent and subordinate relative to the necessary working-out of a trans-historical and trans-individual human purpose.

This tendency to disregard the manifold forms of human thought and activity is continued in Schelling's philosophy. Whereas Fichte insists that individuals can only approximate to the Absolute via action of a moral or practical kind, Schelling regards the self-identification of individuals with the Absolute in terms of their intellectual assimilation to its basic structures. The 'finite' world of human thought and activity therefore comes to be viewed as no more than an illusory reflection of the Absolute rather than as the necessary ground or vehicle of its self-constitution and realization.

It was for this reason, in fact, that Hegel argued that Schelling lacked a proper understanding of the relationship between the existence of the Absolute in its aspect as substance (the 'system of pure reason') and its existence in its aspect as subject (as an active, dynamic impulse to attain concrete existence). According to Hegel, the Absolute must be understood as realized only in so far as it is both substance and subject, both 'in-itself' and 'for-itself', both essence and form. Since Concept or Idea is only actualized in the form of existence, its progress cannot be grasped by a logic that abstracts from the history of its development in successive forms of consciousness, but only by a phenomenology that takes it through all its sequential stages. If this is true, then the phenomenology of the historical dialectic can only be completed at the point where the Absolute itself has completed its progression to ultimate self-realization – a point coincident with the ending of history itself.

Hegel's thought is an attempt to reconcile the tensions preserved in Kant's philosophy and supposedly, but not actually, resolved in Fichtean and Schellingian idealisms: to respect the transcendence of human rationality and purpose over the actual historical and contingent realms of activity and self-realization, without denying the heterogeneity and specificity of actual, concrete existence. For Hegel, each moment of history is conserved in its negation by a Spirit or Consciousness that comes to understand its 'alien' or objective status as an essential stage on the path to self-knowledge. 'Contingent' existence in all its manifold, historical existence is, in fact, necessary from the standpoint of the realization of the Absolute Idea; it is essential to the process of Spirit's self-transcendence, and preserved within it.

The brilliance and originality of this conception lies in the fact that the transcendent Absolute which is the subject of this process of self-realization through successive 'alienations' is also continuously its own object: it has to include its own 'thought-activity' as part of the process whereby it is established. According to Hegel, therefore, the evolution of human Reason is essential to the evolution of the Absolute Idea and does not represent some separate and merely contingent order of reality. Hegel, as has been said, is 'not writing about the Mind: he is writing the Mind's autobiography'.[2]

It is for this reason that we can speak of Hegel's philosophy as a 'humanism'. His 'phenomenology' is intended to reveal the truth of the soul, or consciousness, which is the object of anthropological understanding. Hegel none the less repudiates any notion of the human essence as pre-given, and it is in this light that we must appreciate his influence upon the development of the humanisms associated with Marxism and existentialism, both of which attempt to think humanistically within a framework that is critical of essentialist metaphysics.

The self-realization of Spirit is conceived in terms of its attempt to 'cancel' the objectivity of its objective existence through the assimilation of it to itself. It is this endeavour which Hegel theorizes in the Master–Slave dialectic: consciousness exists for itself only when its autonomy is recognized by another consciousness; to be self-aware is to require another who is self-aware to be aware of one's self-awareness. Hence the antagonism of self-consciousnesses to each other, and the schism between 'Master' and 'Slave'.

Paradoxically, however, it is precisely through its forced labour in producing objects for another that the Slave consciousness is able to contemplate itself in its own exteriorization – and is thus set on the path to the negation of its own unfreedom. Servitude and abstinence – human alienation in labour – is thus regarded by Hegel as a necessary stage in the realization of the essential spirituality of humanity.

The implication of the Master–Slave dialectic is that the clashes of actual human history do not ultimately conflict with the goal towards which it is tending. Reality, in Hegel's conception, is at odds with what is rational only at an immature stage of evolution of thought – a stage at which it has not yet come to appreciate the role of the existing world in the constitution of rationality. Such a viewpoint, however, is clearly open to differing interpretations. In positing the ultimate realization of the Absolute Idea, the ultimate coincidence, in other words, of Being with its Concept, Hegel obviously hopes to rescue philosophy from the question of the *relationship* of thought to being. He aims to transcend the distinction between necessity and freedom, between the finitude of the world and the infinity of Spirit. But does he manage to overcome these dualisms – to retain, in opposition to Kant, the essential unity of fact and value, of the natural and the human – only at the cost of sacrificing any criteria by which we might assess the rationality of the historical process? Does Hegel see everything that happens in history – however capricious, brutal or 'inhumane' – as an immanent part of the process by which the essence of humanity is brought into being, and in that sense as implicitly 'human' and therefore just? Would he have us justify everything simply *because it has come to pass*? Or does he mean that we are able as rational beings to assess the course of history in the light of what we take to be reasonable and that we therefore have a duty to render reality consistent with what we judge to be progressive? Does the Hegelian system, in other words, invite us to view ourselves as the vehicles by which a trans-individual meaning is gradually unfolded in history, and hence to understand history itself as a 'process without a subject'? Or is Hegel's 'idealism' radically different from that of his predecessors by reason of the manner in which Spirit is conceived as immanent to humanity, as receiving its being or meaning only in and through actual human activity?

These questions are given no unambiguous answer in Hegel's thought. The orthodox approach to Hegel has been to treat him as a conservative thinker, whose political theory was a thinly veiled justification of 'totalitarian' practice, and whose metaphysical system-building was unworthy of much serious attention. Needless to say, it was a rather different interpretation of Hegel that was to prove influential to the development of post-war humanist thinking.

Materialist humanism: Feuerbach and Marx

Hegel had understood that no philosophy could comprehend history if it failed to think beyond the static opposition of subject and object. While acknowledging this insight, Marx condemned Hegel for subordinating reality to thought. Since, according to Marx, Hegel recognizes the world only as an objectified form of thought whose purpose is to promote the self-realization of the Idea, he depicts the developing relationship of subject to object as a process evolving in the service of the Concept rather than as itself determined by an independently existing world. Speculative philosophy presents its own activity of thought as belonging to reality itself. Hence its idealism. Though it strives for a synthesis of subject and object, it ends by ascribing subject in substance: 'the idea', says Marx, 'is made the demiurgos of the Real'.[3] Despite the detailed and extensive account of actual historical estrangement that is given in the *Phenomenology*, human alienation is therefore presented by Hegel as if it were a thought process whose contradictions could be resolved wholly in thought. Marx is also critical of Hegel's complacency about the necessity of alienation. For if Spirit can only realize itself through negation of its own negation, then every negation of human nature must itself assume a positive aspect.

The main influence upon Marx's rethinking of Hegel's account of alienation was, of course, Feuerbach, according to whom Hegelian philosophy is itself alienated because it regards alienation as a process affecting thought or consciousness rather than humanity in its material being. It thus presents concrete, finite existence as a mere reflection of a system of thought which in reality owes its origin to 'Man'. Feuerbach's specific example is Man's alienation in religion, but in his *Theses on the Reform of Philosophy* (1843) he extends his conception of alienation to encompass not only religion but German philosophy, too, as a form of secular theology. In the *Theses* he argues that since Hegel starts and ends with the infinite, the finite – Man – is presented as only a phase in the evolution of a superhuman spirit. Hence speculative philosophy, by concealing the real source of philosophical ideas in Man himself, mimics the alienation wrought by religion. To escape this alienation, philosophy cannot start with the Absolute, but with that which is alienated by it – the essence of Man himself.

According to Feuerbach, therefore, Man is alienated in the system of religion and philosophy whereby he *mediates* what is in fact a direct relationship of 'sensuous intuition' to concrete reality. The 'negation of the negation' is not, as Hegel supposes, the absolute overcoming of such alienation since it is a process that conserves that which it negates – and in doing so retains the reference in thought to its opposite. It is only when we recognize the true character of our relationship to nature as one of *immediate* unity, certainty and truth, that we attain 'positive humanism', a humanism, that is, which is no longer reliant upon the denial of religion for its positive content.

While Marx's unreserved admiration for Feuerbach's attack on Hegelian philosophy was extremely short-lived, he remained powerfully attracted to this particular argument. It is significant, in fact, that while by late 1843 he was already criticizing Feuerbach for the 'abstraction' of his humanism, he is yet prepared to credit him in the *1844 Manuscripts* with being the 'true conqueror of the old philosophy' and to applaud the extent of his achievement in 'opposing to the negation of the negation, which claims to be the absolute positive, the self-supporting positive, positively based on itself' (p. 328).[4]

It is to this argument that Marx appeals when he claims that Hegel's account of the negation of the negation remains 'at the last act – the act of self-reference in alienation' (p. 345): self-consciousness cannot, as Hegel suggests, overcome its objectivity by being '*at home* in its *other-being as such*' (p. 339).[5] It must be freed entirely from that which opposes it. Only in that manner can the 'true' as opposed to the 'pseudo' essence be confirmed in the negation of the negation.

On the same grounds Marx exposes the shortcomings of atheistic humanism, and proceeds to argue that communism conceived as the mere negation of the negation of private property does not represent the goal of human development:

But since for the socialist man the *entire so-called history of the world* is
nothing but the creation of man through human labour, nothing but the
emergence of nature for man, so he has the visible, irrefutable proof of
his *birth* through himself, of his *genesis*. Since the *real existence* of man and
nature has become evident in practice, through sense experience, because
man has thus become evident for man as the being of nature, and nature
for man as the being of man, the question about an *alien* being, about a
being above nature and man – a question which implies the admission of
the unreality of nature and of man – has become impossible in practice.
Atheism, as the denial of this unreality, has no longer any meaning, for
atheism is a *negation of God*, and postulates the *existence of man* through this

negation; but socialism as socialism, no longer stands in any need of such a mediation. It proceeds from the *theoretically and practically sensuous consciousness* of man and of nature as the *essence*. Socialism is man's *positive self-consciousness*, no longer mediated through the abolition of religion, just as *real life* is man's positive reality, no longer mediated through the abolition of private property, through *communism*. Communism is the position as the negation of the negation, and is hence the *actual* phase necessary for the next stage of historical development. *Communism* is the necessary form and the dynamic principle of the immediate future, but communism as such is not the goal of human development, the form of human society (pp. 305–6).

For a brief period, Marx himself appears to have assumed with Feuerbach that a change in consciousness alone was sufficient to ensure the realization of 'positive humanism'. Thus we find him writing in 1843 that

Our whole object can only be – as is also the case in Feuerbach's criticism of religion – to give religious and philosophical questions the form corresponding to man who has become conscious of himself. Hence, our motto must be: reform of consciousness not through dogmas, but by analysing the mystical consciousness that is unintelligible to itself, whether it manifests itself in a religious or a political form (p. 144).

But in the *Contribution to the Critique of Hegel's Philosophy of Law. Introduction*, written a few months later, it is implied that Feuerbach's account is deficient precisely because it assumes that 'reform of consciousness' is all that is needed:

The basis of irreligious criticism is: *Man makes religion*, religion does not make man. But *man* is no abstract being encamped outside the world. Man is *the world of man*, the state, society. This state, this society, produce religion, an *inverted world-consciousness* because they are an *inverted world* (p. 175).

For if it is indeed an 'inverted world' that lies at the source of religious alienation, then de-alienation will require more than a change of attitude or renewal of 'self-confidence', and the role of philosophy must itself therefore be differently conceived: 'the immediate *task of philosophy*, which is at the service of history', writes Marx in the *Introduction*, is to unmask self-estrangement in its *'unholy forms'* now that it has been unmasked in its 'holy' form (p. 176). We might note, furthermore, that it is not

Feuerbach but Hegel whom Marx credits in the *1844 Manuscripts* with exposing, albeit only in its abstract and ahistoric development, the essential nature of this *secular alienation*:

> The *Phenomenology* is, therefore, a hidden, mystifying and still uncertain criticism; but inasmuch as it depicts man's *estrangement*, even though man appears only as mind, there lie concealed in it *all* the elements of criticism, already *prepared* and *elaborated* in a manner often rising far above the Hegelian standpoint. The outstanding achievement of Hegel's *Phenomenology*, and of its final outcome, the dialectic of negativity as the moving and generating principle, is thus first that Hegel conceives the self-creation of man as a process, conceives objectification as loss of the object, as alienation and transcendence of this alienation; that he thus grasps the essence of *labour* and comprehends objective man – true, because real man – as the outcome of man's *own labour*. The *real, active* orientation of man to himself as a species-being . . . is only possible if he really brings out all his *species-powers* – something which in turn is only possible through the co-operative action of all mankind, only as the result of history – and treats these powers as objects: and this, to begin with, is again only possible in the form of estrangement (pp. 332–3).

By 1844, therefore, Marx had come to regard Hegel's dialectic – his understanding of the movement of history – as the essential antidote to Feuerbach's abstract 'religion of love'. He still criticized Hegel for his idealist presentation of alienation:

> It is not the fact that the human being *objectifies himself inhumanly*, in opposition to himself, but the fact that he *objectifies himself* in *distinction* from and in *opposition* to abstract thinking, that constitutes the posited essence of the estrangement and the thing to be superceded. The appropriation of man's essential powers, which have become objects – indeed, alien objects – is thus in the first place only an *appropriation* occurring in *consciousness*, in *pure thought*, i.e. in *abstraction* . . . (p. 331).

But what is positive about his philosophy is that it remains thoroughly 'negative and critical'. Furthermore, it is in terms of Hegelian concepts of 'absolute negativity' and 'transcendence' (concepts which Feuerbach had dismissed as applicable only within the mystified realm of philosophy) that Marx proceeded to define his own 'positive' humanism as a naturalism to be distinguished both from vulgar materialism (with its notion of Communism as the goal of human development) and from idealism; 'consistent naturalism or humanism is distinct from both idealism and materialism, and constitutes at the same time the unifying truth of both' (p. 336).

According to this 'humanism', human beings are *natural beings* – actively or 'subjectively' natural in so far as they possess vital forces or powers, and 'objectively' natural in so far as, like plants or animals, they depend on a nature outside themselves for the expression of their essential powers. It is not, therefore, the *act of positing* their essential powers as alien that is the subject of alienation (as if what was involved was a purely subjective act of objective creation); the subjectivity of the process resides in these essential powers in their objective existence, in the objective production that is 'man's' nature 'outside of himself', his existence as an objective, natural being. 'Man' is alienated, therefore, in 'being posited' by the objects of his natural existence as an objective being. At the same time, Man's nature cannot be reduced either to his subjective sensibility or to his objective activity. Its 'humanly-natural' status is brought into being in and through an historical process of mediation with the 'purely natural'. Humanity, in short, is neither directly co-extensive with nature, nor transcendent to it.

In thus arguing for a humanism that unites idealism and materialism, Marx appears to agree with Feuerbach against Hegel, that the 'negation of the negation' is not the 'absolute positive' (since it represents a 'humanism' still dependent on the stage it has transcended). But he also agrees with Hegel against Feuerbach that there is no immediate unity of humanity and nature.

That which mediates between the natural and the human is certainly not merely thought in its objectified form; but nor is such mediation solely an illusion of speculative philosophy. Feuerbach, it is implied, is rightly critical of the dialectic in its idealistic form – but naïve to assume a direct harmonization of humanity and nature to be possible. Hegel had appreciated the role of human labour in our relations with the natural world – even though he had presented these in mystified form. The mediation of labour could not be bypassed in thought (as Feuerbach imagines when he appeals to direct 'sensuous intuition') but must be worked through in reality. In this sense human labour in the alienated form of its existence under relations of capitalist production is viewed as essential to the realization of 'positive humanism': the transcendence of alienation in the abolition of private property is at the same time the realization of the positive potential of capitalist relations – of the opportunity they create for a truly human existence.

Hegel had therefore been correct, according to Marx, to insist upon the indispensability of concrete activity to the realization of spirit; his mistake lay in his failure to take account of that activity in its 'real' or 'sensuous' aspect. His failure, that is, to differentiate finally between the 'sensuous' object and its concept. The implication of this accusation is that Hegel is only able to effect a reconciliation of humanity and nature by 'spiritualizing' nature – by neglecting nature in its 'brute' materiality. There are some, however, who argue that the 'naturalistic humanism' of Marx's *1844 Manuscripts* is also guilty of 'anthropologizing' nature. They argue, that is, that Marx sees in nature only the vehicle of the realization of the human essence, and regards the material transformation wrought by human practical activity ('*praxis*') as a continuous process of alienation in, and negation of, non-human nature.

The discussion of alienated labour in the *1844 Manuscripts* is certainly less lucid than it might be, but there is little to support the view that Marx regarded every objectification of human labour as a negative or alien form of subjectivity. It is clear, in fact, both from the *Manuscripts* and from other texts, that Marx viewed alienation as specific to bourgeois society, associating it directly with the purely *economic* and impersonal relations of contract and exchange that predominate in the market economy – relations which he contrasts with the rigid, hierarchical, and essentially *political* ordering of feudal society. Individuals in commodity society, being free from personal ties of dependence, come to view themselves as independent economic units who relate to each other only 'accidentally' through the medium of the market. Since, moreover, it is the aim of bourgeois methods of production to accumulate profit for the owners of capital, rather than to satisfy the wants of the mass of workers, it is the commodity rather than the needs it is produced to serve that becomes of the locus of value. Human beings thus come progressively to recognize themselves as having value only in so far as they find an alien reflection in the world of things produced.

Alienation is, therefore, essentially the loss of personal ties to the community, and their replacement by the indirect bond of money. As such, it is contrasted by Marx both with the particular oppression and inflexibility of feudal society and with the emancipation and restoration of community that will follow the abolition of capitalism. Indeed, to view alienation as a permanent feature of human production is, so Marx argues both in the *1844 Manuscripts* and in the *Grundrisse*, precisely the fault of the bourgeois economists. It is they who accept as necessary to human labouring as such the greed, competition, immiseration and monetary values which Marx himself describes as alienating and which he associates with a definite historical form of production.

It is true that Marx presents alienation as engendering private property rather than vice versa. Thus he writes, for example, that 'though private property appears to be the reason, the cause of alienated labour, it is rather its consequence, just as the gods are *originally* not the cause but the effect of man's intellectual confusion' (p. 279–80). But the point here – and it has been made by several commentators[6] – is that Marx is speaking of a structural rather than an historical relationship. His argument is not that alienation precedes private ownership, but that property or capital is *nothing but* alienated labour: the power and value it appears to possess in itself is accountable entirely to the labour power it embodies. Far from denying the historical character of alienation in speaking of it as responsible for private property, therefore, Marx is associating it all the more specifically with capitalist production, with a form of production, that is, in which property relations are themselves created and sustained by the *economic* exploitation of the worker rather than existing in the form of an already instituted political constraint.[7]

Some commentators have been at pains to argue that Marx's concept of alienation is not based on an 'ethical' appeal to an abstract 'essence of man'.[8] Now Marx clearly rejects as 'idealist' the idea of an ahistoric (or trans-historic) essence of humanity which awaits redemption in communist society. It is only thanks to capitalist productive forces, he argues, that we are able in principle to achieve the control over social process which alone makes possible a non-alienated existence.

None the less, the concept of alienation remains ethical, in that Marx uses it to deplore the loss of humanity associated with capitalism. It could also be said to be essentialist in that it allows Marx to regard communism as a more 'truly human' form of existence. Let us add, finally, that the theory of alienation is conceptualized within the framework of a more general theory of human species-being: alienation is presented as a form of unfreedom that can only befall those who possess consciousness. Although Marx tells us that for alienated individuals 'what is animal becomes human and what is human becomes animal' (p. 274), no animal is liable to alienation – because no animal is capable of rationally choosing its mode of existence. The theory of alienation, in short, is rooted in humanist assumptions regarding the potential freedom and constitutive role of human beings in the creation and control of social processes.

In fact, in *The German Ideology* Marx uses the term 'alienation' almost exclusively to describe a situation by which those responsible for the creation and maintenance of a process experience it as if it were a natural phenomenon beyond their control. Very little is said of 'alienation' in relation to labour, and the emphasis is on ways in which individuals are complicit in their own oppression through ignorance of their role in the reproduction of social life. Alienated processes appear to them as if they were natural processes; but unlike the latter, they can be overthrown by humanity activity.

We might note, therefore, that though there is a decisive shift away from Feuerbachian humanism in *The German Ideology*, there is no break with humanist argument as such. In *The German Ideology*, Feuerbach comes under direct attack for his 'essentialist' account of human nature; he is charged with reducing 'real historical man' to a philosophical category; and both he and his 'true' socialist followers are condemned for their purely moral critique of capitalism and their pious invocations of the 'Man' or 'species-being' to be realized in communist society. We may therefore agree that *The German Ideology* and the works that post-date it are 'anti-humanist' if we mean by this to indicate the polemical stance adopted in those texts towards abstract concepts of 'Man' and 'human essence'.

Nevertheless, *The German Ideology* remains profoundly humanist in the stress it lays both on the alienation of bourgeois society and on the role of individuals in making history. Abstract humanism is rejected by Marx and Engels, in fact, not because they have come round to the view that human beings are helpless puppets of forces irretrievably beyond their control, but because they have come to appreciate that it is not a philosophical concept ('Man') that 'makes history', but real individuals in definite historical conditions. As they write:

The individuals, who are no longer subject to the division of labour, have been conceived by the philosophers as an ideal, under the name 'man', and the whole process which we have outlined has been regarded by them as the evolutionary process of 'man', so that at every historical stage 'man' was substituted for the individuals hitherto existing and shown as the motive force of history. The whole process was thus conceived as a process of the self-estrangement (*Selbstentfremdungsprozess*) of 'man', and this was essentially due to the fact that the average individual of the later stage was always foisted on to the individuals of an earlier. Through this inversion, which from the first disregards the actual conditions, it was possible to transform the whole of history into an evolutionary process of consciousness.[9]

The message here is that it is not 'Man' who makes history, but *individuals*. Marx forcibly repeats the point a year later in his attack on Proudhon in *The Poverty of Philosophy*. When, Marx writes, we ask ourselves

. . . why a particular principle was manifested in the eleventh or in the eighteenth rather than in any other century, we are necessarily forced to examine minutely what men were like in the eleventh century, what they were like in the eighteenth, what were their respective needs, their productive forces, their mode of production, the raw materials of their production – in short what were the relations between man and man which resulted from all these conditions of existence. To get to the bottom of all these questions – what is this but to draw up the real, profane history of men in every century and to present these men as *both the authors and the actors of their own drama*?[10]

It is true, of course, that these 'authors and actors' are subsumed in classes and subordinated to forces (the division of labour, exchange relations) with which they have no choice but to comply, and that the products of their own creation therefore acquire an appearance of independence. The 'social power', writes Marx in *The German Ideology*,

which arises through the co-operation of different individuals . . . appears to these individuals, since their co-operation is not voluntary but has come about naturally, not as their united power, but as an alien force existing outside them, of the origin and goal of which they are ignorant, and which they are thus no longer able to control. . . .[11]

Marx and Engels imply that alien forces do in fact determine the will and action of individuals in bourgeois society; that people *do* become mere functionaries in a system of relations apparently possessed of its own dynamic and created independently of those who 'support' it. But it is, of course, precisely for that reason that they aspire to overthrow capitalist relations and speak of the need to replace 'the domination of circumstances and of chance over individuals by the domination of individuals over chance and circumstances'.[12]

From the standpoint, in fact, of the argument of the so-called 'Works of the break',[13] the structuralist reading of Marx must be seen to come under direct attack for presenting an absence of control that is specific to bourgeois existence as an eternal verity: in regarding the relations of capitalist existence as endowed with a life of their own, the structuralist account makes of the 'non-subject' of bourgeois society the non-subject as such – the perpetual subordination of individuals to the structures they unwittingly 'support'.

So little is it true, in fact, that the attack on the critical omnipotence of philosophy in *The German Ideology* amounts to a severance with humanist argument, that we encounter in the text some of Marxist humanism's more problematic theses. The viewpoint, for example, remains strongly teleological: the goal of history is the abolition of bourgeois society and the establishment of communism as the final and completed form of human emancipation. Communism itself is depicted as a society of direct, unmediated relations of 'person to person' in which all forms of State organization and political institutions have disappeared. Its advent is presented as marking the end of politics (necessary only in class societies), and the end of history (that is, the end of antagonistic relations of production). At the same time, it is suggested that with the demise of bourgeois society there begins an epoch distinguished by its explicitly 'humanist' consciousness:

> communism differs from all previous movements in that it overturns the basis of all earlier relations of production and intercourse, and for the first time consciously treats all naturally evolved premises as the creations of hitherto existing men, strips them of their natural character and subjugates them to the power of the united individuals.[14]

We also, of course, encounter in these works the humanist theme of the proletariat as the 'world-historical' agent of universal emancipation. 'Modern universal intercourse', writes Marx,[15] 'cannot be controlled by individuals unless it is controlled by all', and only the working class is in a position to develop the universality essential to the appropriation of the totality of humanity's productive powers.

Let us note, finally, that Marx and Engels repeatedly distinguished their own critique of capitalism from the 'moralism' of the Feuerbachian humanists, Ricardian socialists, Proudhonians and others, precisely on the grounds that they alone had recognized the necessity of capitalism's 'civilizing influence' to the realization of communism. These would-be reformers, they argued, had failed to appreciate the progressive role of industrialization in breaking down limited and fixed forms of the division of labour and in creating the conditions – both human and material – of an abundant gratification. Being nostalgic in its aspirations, the 'utopian socialist' critique of capitalism was necessarily unconstructive and ineffective. It has been suggested that it is precisely because it respects the positive and material legacy of capitalist alienation that the Marxism dialectic differs from that of Hegel:

For Marx the negative inheres in an objective world from which the self is estranged – specifically the alienation of labour produces private property; but private property is by no means 'nothing but' labour in estrangement because the labour becomes *embodied* in *material form* and the material, which is the stuff of the natural form of the commodity, is drawn from the naturally given object of labour.[16]

On the one hand, therefore, the material embodiment of estranged labour is preserved in its 'absolute positivity' (i.e. as the material basis of socialist production) despite the 'negation' of private ownership; on the other hand, in the transition from capitalism to socialism there is an absolute negation of alienating social relations, since these are not conceived from the standpoint of socialism as a conserved 'moment' within its higher unity.

We can agree, however, that Marx himself viewed the material embodiment of alienated labour under capitalism as a 'positive' residue transcending the negation of capitalist social relations, and providing the grounds for future existence, without subscribing in full to his attack upon 'Utopian socialism'. There are, indeed, many socialists who today dispute the Marxist account of transition to socialism on the grounds that it is the productivity unleashed by capitalist methods of production that constitutes the major 'material' obstacle to the socialist transformation of the industrialized nations, and that technological success in dominating nature now directly threatens the project of human emancipation. Since the 'wealth' generated by capitalist production is ecologically unsustainable, pre-emptive of genuine human satisfaction, and disastrous in its consequences for the vast majority of people inhabiting the globe today, it is the basic conditions of existence of 'advanced' civilization that must be overhauled if any 'socialism' worthy of the name is to be realized. In the words of Rudolf Bahro:

Our customary idea of the transition to socialism is the abolition of the capitalist order within the basic conditions European civilisation has created in the field of technique and technology – and not in Europe alone. Even in this century, a thinker as profound as Antonio Gramsci was still able to view technique, industrialisation, Americanism, the Ford system in its existing form as by and large an inescapable necessity, and thus depict socialism as the genuine executor of human adaptation to modern machinery and technology. Marxists have so far rarely considered that humanity has not only to transform its relations of production, but must also fundamentally transform the entire character of its mode of production, i.e. the productive forces, the so-called technostructure. It must not see its perspective as bound up with any historically transmitted form of the development of needs and their satisfaction, or of the world of products designed for that purpose. The commodity world that we find around us is not in its present form a necessary condition of human existence. It does not have to look the way it does in order for human beings to develop both intellectually and emotionally as far as we would like.[17]

For such a viewpoint, that which Marx took to be the grounds of our escape from alienation – the material embodiment of estranged labour that is preserved in the 'absolute positivity' of socialist relations – is itself a primary source of alienation.

Marxist humanist thought in the 1920s

Industrialization and technology have, of course, been criticized often enough in the name of Marxism itself, especially by those who have wanted to oppose a 'humanist' to a positivist and deterministic interpretation of historical materialism.

The earliest of these interpretations was that of Georg Lukács in *History and Class Consciousness* (1923), which remains the 'classic' of post-Marx Marxist humanism. To understand the nature and importance – both at the time of publication and subsequently – of Lukács's work (as indeed of that of the other two major 'humanist' Marxists of the 1920s, Antonio

Gramsci and Karl Korsch), it is essential to realize that Marx's early 'humanist' writings were almost entirely unknown to the first generation of Marxist theoreticians in the Second International. Neither the *1844 Manuscripts* nor *The German Ideology* had been published; Engels's account of Marx's early formation in *Ludwig Feuerbach and the End of Classical German Philosophy* (1888) remained the unchallenged authority; and in ignorance of the early philosophical input, Marxist scholars came to identify Marxism with the economic and political theory to be found in *Capital* and other published works, a theory to which they brought a decidedly positivistic interpretation. It is with some justice, therefore, that Lucien Goldmann has written:

The origins of existentialism date back at least to Kierkegaard, and dialectical thought was of course first systematically elaborated by Hegel, to take on a materialist form with Marx and Engels. And yet, between Kierkegaard, Hegel and Marx on the one hand, and the existentialist and Marxist works of Lukács on the other (*The Soul and the Forms*, 1911 and *History and Class Consciousness*, 1923) runs a long period of positivist thought which has dominated western European philosophy, so that the appearance of these two books must be regarded as a veritable renaissance. In this sense, and with this reservation, it is not incorrect to say that between 1910 and 1925 a true philosophical turning-point occurred, which resulted in the creation of existentialism and contemporary dialectical materialism.[18]

For Lukács, the rediscovery of Marx the 'dialectician' was in a very real and important sense the rediscovery of Marx the 'Hegelian', since he argued (contrary to the orthodox opinion), that Marx had arrived at his materialist theory of history not by rejecting Hegelian philosophy, but by defending its central categories of 'totality' and 'subject–object identity' against the 'critical criticism' of the Neo-Hegelians. In a sense, in fact, Marx had to be seen as more consistently Hegelian than Hegel, since in arguing that history is the work of the Absolute Idea Hegel had in effect introduced a standpoint external to the totality of being and consciousness and had thus made it too easy for the Neo-Hegelians to return to a Kantian dualism in which a 'critical consciousness' (the Idea or 'subject' of history) was opposed to the real world ('object') it was condemning. Marx, by contrast, according to Lukács, remained committed to the unity of thought and being, and thus to the immanence of critique within the totality, when he rejected both idealism and its foil in mechanical materialism.

It is, in short, not Marx's insistence upon the primacy of economic determinations that distinguishes his thought from bourgeois science and philosophy, but his dialectical rejection of every subject–object dualism. Elaborating on Marx's concept of commodity fetishism in *Capital*, Lukács presents a theory of the 'reification' to which bourgeois society succumbs as a result of its relations of production: in a society where value is thought to be immanent in things, and persons themselves regarded as commodities, the role of human action in the creation of social meaning is lost to view. Science treats the productions of human *praxis* as purely factual, and philosophy endorses the supposed neutrality of science. In this situation, according to Lukács, only the proletariat – because it alone of all classes aims to abolish itself rather than to defend its partial interests – is able to arrive at a consciousness of the totality and thus to transcend reification. The proletariat is the 'identical subject–object' of the historical process, which through the negation of its own negation, will accomplish the emancipation of humankind as a whole.

In attacking the objectivity of science, Lukács has been charged by his critics with undermining the claims to scientificity of Marxism itself, and with misrepresenting Marx's own account of capitalist society. Gareth Stedman Jones, for example, has deplored *History and Class Consciousness* as the 'first major irruption of the romantic anti-scientific tradition of bourgeois thought into Marxist theory', arguing that Lukács so far abstracts from Marx's recognition of the 'civilizing influence' of capitalism as to see in the theory of alienation a condemnation of industrialization as such. Lukács attack on science, claims Stedman Jones, owes nothing to Marx but is inspired by Weber, Dilthey and the 'Heidelberg' school of German anti-positivism in which Lukács received his first philosophical training: it is Weber's horror of the 'little cogs' produced by capitalist rationalization that lies behind the concept of 'reification', and the nostalgic *Lebensphilosophie* of Simmel and Bergson that led Lukács to overlook Marx's approval of science and his insistence upon the necessity of industrialization to de-alienation.[19]

Yet if *History and Class Consciousness* was less than faithful to Marx's pronouncements on science, it anticipated in an almost uncanny way many of the humanist themes that were to be revealed as 'also Marxist' with the publication in 1932 of the *1844 Manuscripts*. When interest in Marx the humanist became extensive after 1945, it was to Lukács above all that post-war Marxists turned for interpretative guidelines.

While closer to classical Marxism in his attitude to science, and less inclined than Lukács to play down the role of economic forces or to abstract from questions of political strategy, Karl Korsch's reading of Marxism shared much in common with that of Lukács. In the afterword to his major work, *Marxism and Philosophy* (1923), Korsch in fact professed himself in basic agreement with the argument of *History and Class Consciousness*. Outspoken in his criticism of the Marxism of the Second International, he called for a renewal of Marxist philosophy and emphasized the need for an integrated philosophical–economic–political theory of social development in its totality.

Also extremely important to the construction of a humanist understanding of Marxism in the inter-war years was the work of Antonio Gramsci. Insisting, like Lukács, on Marx's debt to Hegel, Gramsci argued that Marx had transcended both traditional materialism and traditional idealism in founding a 'philosophy of *praxis*' that was conceived in immanentist terms but purified of all speculative or metaphysical overtones. The philosophy of *praxis*, according to Gramsci, is an 'absolute "historicism"', the absolute secularisation and earthliness of thought, the absolute humanism of history';[20] it is, that is to say, a non-metaphysical 'faith' or 'conception of the world' that is truly humanist because it is the conception that is manifested in the practical activity of its time. It is worth noting that Gramsci's 'humanist' Marxism has always been opposed in his native Italy, particularly through the work of Della Volpe which has dominated the development of post-war Italian Marxism.

Hegel, phenomenology and existentialism: the influence of Alexandre Kojève

If, as Roger Garaudy has claimed, Lukács had fostered the view of Hegel as a Marxist *'avant la lettre'*,[21] Alexandre Kojève was to further the acceptance of Hegelian philosophy by the existentialists by reading Hegel as a Husserlian *'avant la lettre'*.[22] Edmund Husserl, we might note, had been a prominent figure in the Heidelberg school from which Lukács had drawn inspiration for his defence of the Hegelian subject–object identity. Kojève took the process further arguing that Hegel was 'realist' *because* Husserlian. Hegel was by no means an idealist, he argued, in lectures delivered in 1933-9 at the *École Practique des Hautes Études*; his philosophy is dialectical not because he (idealistically) employs a dialectical method, but because Being itself is dialectical and Hegel's thought represents this reality. In so far as Hegel can be said to have a method, therefore, it is 'purely contemplative and descriptive, or better, phenomenological in Husserl's sense of the term' (p. 171).[23]

In his interpretation of the concluding paragraph of the *Phenomenology of Spirit*, Kojève insists that Hegel's Spirit must be understood in realist-existentialist terms as a revealed Being, a true synthesis of (objective) Being and its (subjective) revelation. It is not therefore an *a priori*, predetermining point of origin, but a result arrived at *a posteriori*; in contrast to the idealism of Fichte and Schelling, Hegel's dialectic of Subject and Object is meaningful precisely because it involves the existence of an Object 'properly so-called – that is an object external to and independent of the Subject' (p. 152). The object, in Hegel's philosophy, is thus to be given (as indeed Hegel claims it should) its 'full freedom' (*seine völlige Freiheit*).

In this manner, Kojève arrives at an interpretation of Hegel which gives prominence to the activity and creativity of the Object (history-reality) in the production of a Spirit that is 'contingent and free' – whose necessary path of becoming can be reconstructed with hindsight though not foreseen in advance. There is thus no transcendent Spirit – or meaning – standing outside the human historical world. 'The Spirit is nothing but the historical becoming of Man' (p. 162). Hegel's *Phenomenology* is therefore first and foremost an empirical anthropology: an interpretation of historical events in terms of their human meaning. 'The temporal past of eternal Being is *human* and only human', claims Kojève. Thus

> The *Phenomenology* ends with a radical denial of all transcendence . . . the Infinite in question is *Man's* infinite. Hence the 'Science' that reveals this infinite-Being is a Science of Man in two ways: on the one hand it is the result of history – that is, a product of Man; and on the other, it talks about Man: about *his* temporal or historical becoming (p. 167).

Kojève's only real criticism of Hegel is that he fell into confusion by identifying a dialectic in nature as well as in human history. In every other respect, Hegel's philosophy represents a thoroughgoing humanism:

an exercise in the revelation of true humanity, of what distinguishes 'Culture', 'Man' and 'History' from 'Animal' and 'Nature'. Though he admits that in the *Encyclopedia* Hegel is ambiguous about the dialectical character of Nature, and that even the *Phenomenology* is marred by vacillation on that issue, Kojève none the less insists that we should 'abstract' from this error (p. 215f.), and commit ourselves wholeheartedly to the dualism of Man and Nature. For Hegel's brilliance lies in seeing that humanity's difference from the natural world – a difference which must be respected in philosophical dualism – concerns the specific form of human Desire. It is the specificity of this 'anthropogenetic' Desire ('Desire for the Other's Desire – for the Other's recognition') that Kojève claims is theorized in Hegel's chapter on the Master–Slave dialectic.[24]

Most of the themes we associate with French existentialism: ontological dualism, and the denial of the dialectics of nature; the conception of human being as nothingness; the identification of action with nihilation; a phenomenological humanism rooted in the idea that human desire cannot be conceived in terms of a traditional category of essence, because it essentially lacks an essence – all these are themes which Kojève finds prefigured if not definitely theorized in Hegel's work.

But while Kojève's development of an existentialist neo-Hegelianism helps us to understand why it was to Hegel and to an Hegelianized form of Marxism that existentialist philosophers such as Sartre and Merleau-Ponty first turned, in an effort to politicize existentialist philosophy, the fact remains that it is hard to reconcile the existentialist concern with individual experience with Hegel's invitation to us to look down from the plateau of Absolute Knowledge and Freedom upon the 'gnats of subjectivity' being consumed in the 'devouring flame' of the Eternal.[25]

Acknowledging this, Kojève's contemporary, Jean Hyppolite, argued that despite the existentialist elements in Hegel's thought, the *Phenomenology* culminates in a subordination of the individual to the universal.[26] Nor did Sartre and Merleau-Ponty nourish many illusions about the extent of the clash between 'orthodox' Hegel and their own philosophy.

Indeed, if one regards Kierkegaard as the 'founder' of existentialism, then its roots lie in a reaction against Hegel. For Kierkegaard typifies the extreme humanist–individualist rejection of Hegelian rationality, and in asserting, as Sartre puts it in the *Problem of Method*, 'the narrow, passionate, intransigence of immediate life against the tranquil meditation of all reality', Kierkegaardian existentialism constituted a resistance to any systematic philosophy at all. The 'humanism' of the Kierkegaardian pole of existentialism thus denies the very possibility of a 'philosophy of existence', on the grounds that life is untheorizably unique. Discussing Kierkegaard's antagonism to Hegel, Sartre writes:

In fact, the subjective life, just insofar as it is lived, can never be made the object of a knowledge. In principle it escapes knowing, and the relation of the believer to transcendence can only be conceived of in a form of *going beyond*. This inwardness, which in its narrowness and its infinite depth claims to affirm itself against all philosophy, this subjectivity rediscovered beyond language as the personal adventure of each man in the face of others and of God – this is what Kierkegaard called existence.[27]

According to Sartre, however, the problem with such subjectivism is that in emphasizing the uniqueness of individual existence, it may re-establish a philosophy of transcendence: abstracting too much from the social context, it tends to favour 'inner' mental adjustment to an uncomprehended and offensive 'outer' reality. Though it starts 'humanistically' from 'needs, griefs, passions and pains', it ends in a rejection of the concrete, and instead either adopts an attitude of pessimistic contemplation or seeks solace in the transcendence of religion. This is the charge that Sartre makes against Kierkegaard and pessimistic or theological existentialism in general.

What was needed instead, according to Sartre, was a form of existentialism which would be able to sustain Kierkegaard's basic assertion, against Hegel, of the irreducibility of the human subject, but which was at the same time able to accommodate the social and material context of individual existence. For those who, like Sartre and Merleau-Ponty, sought to establish existentialism as a secular philosophy of action, there could be no resort to religion. Existentialists who hoped to 'solve' the question of relations with others – and by extension of participation in the world – by concentrating purely upon the intransigent uniqueness of individual life, were evading the real issue, which was the tension between respect for individuality and the need to act in a common situation for social ends.

Notes

1 This is the central theme of an address 'On the Dignity of Man' written in 1794. For a discussion of Fichte's philosophy and his influence on the development of Marxism, see Leszek Kalakowski, *Main Currents of Marxism*, vol. I (Oxford 1978), pp. 50-6. Roger Garaudy emphasizes Marx's debt to Fichte in *Karl Marx, the evolution of his thought* (London 1964), pp. 33-43.
2 Kolakowski, *Main Currents of Marxism*, p. 60.
3 Karl Marx, *Capital*, vol. I (London 1974), p. 29.
4 Page numbers here and in the following pages refer to Karl Marx/Frederick Engels, *Collected Works* (hereafter *CW*) (London 1975-   ), vol. 3.
5 Georg F. W. Hegel, *Phenomenology of Spirit* (Oxford 1977), para. 788.
6 See David McLellan, *Marx before Marxism* (Harmondsworth 1970), p. 224; Chris Arthur, *The German Ideology*, part 1 (London 1970), pp. 17-18, and 'Hegel, Feuerbach, Marx and Negativity', *Radical Philosophy*, no. 35 (autumn 1983).
7 In other words, property relations under feudalism are not sustained, as they are under capitalism, by the process of exploitation itself, but are directly political in character. See Chris Arthur, *The German Ideology*, p. 11.
8 In 'Marx and the Critique of Political Economy', *Ideology in Social Science*, ed. Robin Blackburn (London 1972), p. 289, Norman Geras, for example, has argued:

Here (in *Capital*), the roots of the phenomena grouped under the term alienation, are located in specific social relations, and not in the fact that there is an ideal essence of man, his 'species-being', which has been negated or denied. . . . In place of the concept of alienation founded on an essentialist anthropology, we have one tied to the historical specificity of forms of domination.

But, as we have seen, alienation is theorized as specific to capitalism already in the *1844 Manuscripts*. The real issue concerns the reliance of the theory on the concept of the 'truly human' rather than its historical specificity. Since Geras has recently argued for the presence in Marxism of a theory of human nature (see *Marx and Human Nature, Refutation of a Legend* (London 1983)) he presumably no longer feels

that Marx's theory needs to be rescued from imputations of essentialism.
9 *CW*, vol. 5, pp. 88-9 and p. 77.
10 *CW*, vol. 6, p. 170 (my emphasis).
11 *CW*, vol. 5, pp. 88-9; see also Marx's discussion in *Capital* of the way in which the trans-individual power generated by the 'collective worker' is mistakenly attributed to capitalist production. Since the workers, he says (Marx, *Capital*, vol. I, pp. 314-15), view their union into a single body and the establishment of a connection between their individual functions, as 'matters foreign and external to them', they credit capital with bringing into being a force they themselves have generated in reality. As regards the use of the term 'alienation' in *The German Ideology*, it is clear that reluctant as Marx is, as he says, to employ a concept 'comprehensible only to the philosopher', it remains the only one available to him to express the particular fixity or consolidation of social activity in bourgeois society to which he wishes to draw attention.
12 *CW*, vol. 5, p. 438.
13 This is Louis Althusser's term for works written during the period 1845-6.
14 *CW*, vol. 5, p. 81.
15 *CW*, vol. 5, p. 88.
16 Chris Arthur, *The German Ideology*, p. 17.
17 Rudolf Bahro, *Socialism and Survival* (London 1982), p. 27.
18 Lucien Goldmann, *Lukács and Heidegger* (London 1977), p. 4.
19 Gareth Stedman Jones, 'The Marxism of the Early Lukács', *Western Marxism*, edited by *New Left Review* (London 1977), p. 33.
20 Antonio Gramsci, *Il materialismo storico e la filosofia di Benedetto Croce* (Milan 1948), p. 159. In affirming Hegel's influence upon Marx, Gramsci was himself influenced by Croce's philosophy.
21 Roger Garaudy, *Dieu est Mort. Étude sur Hegel* (Paris 1962), p. 413.
22 For a discussion of the influence of Alexandre Kojève on contemporary French philosophy, see Vincent Descombes, *Modern French Philosophy* (Cambridge 1980), pp. 9-16 and pp. 27-48; David Archard, *Marxism and Existentialism* (Belfast 1980), pp. 4-6.
23 Page numbers here and in the following pages refer to Alexandre Kojève, *Introduction to the Reading of Hegel* (London 1969; first published in French, Paris 1947), p. 171.

24 Man's humanity 'comes to light' only in risking his life to satisfy his human Desire. Now to desire a Desire is to want to substitute oneself for the value desired by this Desire. For without this substitution, one would desire the value, the desired object, and not Desire itself. Therefore . . . human anthropogenetic Desire – the Desire that generates Self-consciousness, the human reality – is finally, a function of the desire for 'recognition'. And the risk of life by which the human reality 'comes to light' is a risk for the sake of such a Desire. Therefore, to speak of the 'origin' of Self-consciousness is necessarily to speak of a fight to the death for 'recognition'. Without this fight to the death for pure prestige, there would never have been human beings on earth (ibid., p. 7).

In treating the Master–Slave dialectic as a discourse concerning the origin of humanity, as concerned, that is, with the triumph of an essentially *human* desire over a merely animal desire for preservation, the 'humanist' or 'anthropologistic' bias of Kojève's reading of Hegel is very obvious. Marx, we might note, never mentioned the Master–Slave dialectic. See Chris Arthur, 'Hegel's Master–Slave Dialectic and a Myth of Marxology', *New Left Review*, no. 142 (November–December 1983).

25 The reference is to a passage from an early essay (*Glauben und Wissen* 1802). It is cited by Kojève himself (p. 168) as a conclusion to his commentary on the *Phenomenology*, in the course of which he remarks on the depths of depression into which Hegel was thrown by having to acknowledge the 'abandonment of Individuality – that is, actually, of humanity – which the idea of absolute Knowledge demanded'.

26 Jean Hyppolite, 'L'existence dans la "Phenomenologie" de Hegel', in *Figures de la Pensée Philosophique*, vol. I (Paris 1971), pp. 92–103.

27 Jean-Paul Sartre, *Problem of Method* (London 1961), p. 11.

Further reading

The main source texts for the argument of Hegel, Feuerbach and Marx discussed in this chapter are: Georg F. W. Hegel, *Phenomenology of Spirit*, trans. A. V. Miller (Oxford 1977); Ludwig Feuerbach, *The Essence of Christianity*, trans. Marian Evans (George Eliot) (London 1842) (and see also *The Fiery Brook–Selected Writings of Ludwig Feuerbach*, trans. and ed. Z. Hanfi (New York 1972)); Karl Marx, 'Contribution to the Critique of Hegel's Philosophy of Law. Introduction'; 'On the Jewish Question';

'Economic and Philosophical Manuscripts of 1844' – all included in Karl Marx, Friedrich Engels, *Collected Works* (London 1975–) (*CW*), vol. 3; Karl Marx and Friedrich Engels, *The German Ideology*, *CW*, vol. 5. For the 'humanist' Marxism of the inter-war period, see: Georg Lukács, *History and Class Consciousness*, trans. Rodney Livingstone (London 1971); Karl Korsch, *Marxism and Philosophy*, trans. Fred Halliday (London 1970); Antonio Gramsci, *Selections from the Prison Notebooks*, ed. and trans. Quintin Hoare and Geoffrey Nowell Smith (London 1971); Alexandre Kojève's commentary on Hegel's *Phenomenology* is to be found in *Introduction to the Reading of Hegel* (London 1969). For a sense of Jean Hyppolite's contribution to French Neo-Hegelianism, see *Studies on Marx and Hegel* (1955), ed. and trans. John O'Neill (New York 1969); and Henri Lefebvre, *Dialectical Materialism* (1949), trans. John Sturrock (London 1968).

For general accounts of Marx's early philosophical development, see Roger Garaudy, *Karl Marx: The Evolution of His Thought*, trans. Nan Apotheker (London 1967); Leszek Kolakowski, *Main Currents of Marxism* (Oxford 1978), vol. I; Shlomo Avineri, *The Social and Political Thought of Karl Marx* (Cambridge 1968); David McLellan, *The Young Hegelians and Karl Marx* (London 1969) and *Marx Before Marxism* (Harmondsworth 1970). A more detailed charting of the philosophical formation of both Marx and Engels is to be found in Georges Labica, *Marxism and the Status of Philosophy*, trans. Kate Soper and Martin H. Ryle (Brighton 1980). A scholarly and illuminating discussion of the relations between Hegel, Feuerbach and Marx on the question of 'alienation' is to be found in a series of articles by Chris Arthur (see 'Personality and the Dialectic of Labour and Property: Locke, Hegel, Marx', *Radical Philosophy*, no. 26 (autumn 1980); 'Objectification and Alienation in Marx and Hegel', *Radical Philosophy*, no. 30 (spring 1982); 'Hegel, Feuerbach, Marx and Negativity', *Radical Philosophy*, no. 35 (autumn 1983)).

It has been impossible, for reasons of space, to include consideration in this work of the 'critical theory' associated with the members of the Frankfurt Institute of Social Research. But in their critique of positivism, their emphasis on *praxis* and their 'progressive' reading of Hegel, the Frankfurt school theorists do have definite affinities with the French humanists. For comparison with French Neo-Hegelianism, see Herbert Marcuse's *Reason and Revolution: Hegel and the Rise of Social Theory* (1941) (rev. edn Boston 1960); see also 'On the Problem of the Dialectic' (1930), trans. in *Telos*, no. 27 (spring 1976), and 'On the Philosophical

Foundations of the concept of labour in Economics' (1933), trans. in *Telos*, no. 16 (summer 1973). Also relevant is Alfred Schmidt, *The Concept of Nature in Marx* (1962), trans. Ben Fowkes (London 1971); David Held, *Introduction to Critical Theory* (London 1980), chs 6, 7 and 8; and Martin Jay, *The Dialectical Imagination* (London 1973), ch. 2.

For Sören Kierkegaard's existentialism, see *Fear and Trembling and The Sickness unto Death*, trans. Walter Lowrie (Princeton 1954).

3
Philosophical anthropology II – phenomenology and existentialism

The fundamental problem addressed by contemporary humanist thought is that of the inseparability of the human subject from the world, the problem which Lukács referred to as the 'subject–object identity'. As we have seen, it is the refusal to interpret Hegel's Spirit as a transcendent Subject of 'objective' historical reality that is the distinguishing mark of Kojève's 'humanist' reading of Hegel. For Kojève insists that Hegel conceives historical meaning as brought into being only through the activity of empirical human beings, who are at every stage both subjects and objects of the historical process. It is likewise central to Marx's humanist argument that human beings are a part of, and in that sense 'produced' by the reality that they themselves create: the objectivity that confronts us as the condition of our subjectivity is brought into being through a subjective act of objectification. For phenomenology, too, the interdependency of subject and object is the cardinal tenet, requiring, so it is argued, the rejection of both rationalist and empiricist epistemologies – of the former because it relies on a transcendent 'constitutive' subject of consciousness, of the latter because it posits the transcendency of the object to a subject conceived as a merely passive recipient of 'ideas' or 'impressions'. There is no consciousness that is not 'intentional', i.e., consciousness *of something*, and therefore dependent upon the world; equally, however, there is no noumenal realm or thing-in-itself, no meaning to be given, in other words, to the idea of knowledge of an object wholly independent of the subject. Positivism must therefore be rejected, since the idea of an 'objective Science' rests on the assumption of a divorce between the scientist as 'knower' and the object of investigation as existing 'in-itself'.

Edmund Husserl

According to the 'founder' of phenomenology, Edmund Husserl, the true meaning of the world could only emerge in a philosophy which avoided both the 'rationalist' reduction of questions concerning the nature of objects to questions concerning the nature of thought, and the 'empiricist' blindness to the ontological assumptions involved in all knowledge. The intended objects of consciousness had, therefore, to be described in their own terms, as 'phenomena' presenting themselves to a consciousness that was itself an 'outwardness' to them, a direct reflection upon them.

But for such an investigation to be possible, it was necessary, Husserl claimed, for the investigator to 'bracket-off' all theories, ontological presuppositions and evidence for existence – in a manner not dissimilar to Descartes's hyperbolic doubt, but far more radical since it included individual existence within its scope.

Husserlian phenomenology claimed to restore the 'in-the-worldness' of the human subject. Yet Husserl conceived its programme – which he came to argue should be directed at a rigorous and 'scientific'[1] understanding of the 'life-world' (the immediately experienced, subjective and relative world presupposed by all 'objective science') – as itself an exercise in transcendental philosophy: it involved a quest for the subjective conditions of the possibility of an objectively experienceable and knowable world. What Husserl appears to advocate, therefore, is not so much the abandonment of Kantian 'transcendental subjectivity' as its radicalization. It is a question of extending the search for subjective conditions of experience to the 'life-world' which is as 'naïvely' presupposed by Kant in his philosophizing as it is by Einstein in his experimentation. Husserl argued, in fact, that the phenomenological investigation of consciousness discovered it to have distinctive properties and structures, presided over by an 'I' or subject which is as essential to it as are its intended objects. This 'ego' is, of course, distinct from the 'empirical' ego, which is already bracketed off in the *épochè*; it is, in short, transcendental.

Yet how can an ego-endowed consciousness also be an intended consciousness? How can such an ego be conscious of itself as intended (and therefore independent and undifferentiated) consciousness? Husserl's answer is that there must be some intermediary 'stuff' (*hyle*) combining the properties of both ego and objects, and 'contained' in consciousness while at the same time 'representing' the objects intended by the ego. But if the objects of consciousness are 'represented' by it they are no longer strictly speaking 'intended'; nor does consciousness 'directly reflect' them. So it would seem that 'phenomenology' will revert to a Kantian study of the principles by which the objects of consciousness are constituted through the activity of the mind. And so, according to his critics – and these included his pupil, Heidegger – Husserl failed, like Kant, to 'break out into the world', and ended by imprisoning himself again within the subject.

The implication of the method of *épochè* is that the individual can, in principle, abstract from every influence of culture and environment. At the same time, however, Husserl claims that 'to be human . . . is essentially to be a human being in a socially and generatively united civilisation . . .' and that 'if man is a rational being, it is only insofar as his whole civilisation is a rational civilisation . . .'.[2] But this suggests that we are necessarily social and historic beings and therefore incapable of the presuppositionless state of *épochè*. Indeed, this problem of historicity seems posed by Husserl's basic concept of the 'life-world' as that which provides the ground of 'objective science': the 'truths' of 'objective science' are valid, he suggests, only in relation to the 'subjective-relative' nature of 'life'. But if all 'science' is embedded within the life-world and derives its validity from it, is there any 'objective' knowledge at which we can hope to arrive? This question applies, moreover, to philosophy itself, including phenomenology.

Hence the tensions in Husserl's later work between a concern to accommodate the historicity of culture and a desire to establish the meaning of the world 'as such'. Hence, too, the conflict between his highly abstract (and deplorably Eurocentric) pronouncements on 'Man' and the *telos* of civilization, and his recognition that the whole idea of an overall human truth or purpose might be merely fanciful. And yet no sooner has he raised this question of humanity's *telos*, than Husserl argues that it can – indeed will – be settled, and by a purely metaphysical rather than historical investigation. Only philosophy, he writes

Can decide whether the *telos* which was inborn in European humanity at the birth of Greek philosophy – that of humanity which seeks to exist, and is only possible, through philosophical reason, moving endlessly from latent to manifest reason and forever seeking its own norms through this, its truth and genuine human nature – whether this *telos*, then, is merely a factual, historical delusion, the accidental acquisition of merely one among many other civilisations and histories, or whether Greek humanity was not rather the first breakthrough to what is essential to humanity as such, its *entelechy*.[3]

Since, moreover, Husserl goes on immediately to speak of the 'special vocation' of the philosophical community (or, at least, of a certain élite within it) to act as 'functionaries' of the realization of humanity's truth, he appears to have abandoned the impartiality of phenomenological investigation in favour of a more Hegelian philosophy of politics. Whereas Hegel, however, never made the mistake of assuming that the sole significant events of European history were its philosophical theories, Husserl often writes as if he supposed that the only struggles that contribute to humanity's realization are between the rival theories of the western philosophical tradition.

Martin Heidegger

Adopting the method of Husserl's phenomenology, but rejecting what he regarded as its transcendental idealism, Heidegger argued for an 'existentialist' philosophy which would register the 'in-the-worldness' of the human individual and refused primacy to the subject of that world. According to Heidegger, all dualisms of subject and object, consciousness and being, humanity and nature, are a secondary and 'inauthentic' derivation from the primary unity of Being (*Sein*) with human Being (*Dasein*). Humanity and the world form a whole. In Heidegger's philosophy, therefore, the focus shifts from the role of consciousness 'intending' the object, towards the world as, so to speak, 'already intended'. Being, though it finds expression in the manifold entities comprising the world, only 'appears' in so far as it is humanly recognized and understood. For there is, in fact, no primary 'thing-in-itself', but only a 'readiness-to-hand' – the existence of the world as it serves a human purpose. We cannot, Heidegger suggests, authentically regard objects as things; we must see them in terms of our own concerns. Objects only become 'mere' things when some accident forces them on our attention, as when they break down or become unusable. The world comes to us as already meaningful, and human projects are therefore fundamental to ontology.

This means that for Heidegger (as for Lukács),[4] there can be no objective understanding of history, and to suppose otherwise is to succumb to 'inauthenticity' – to be oblivious to the true nature of Being, to approach it as 'thing-like', as meaningless factuality. For Heidegger, however – and this distinguishes his position from any Marxist theory of alienation/reification – 'inauthenticity' is not the product of definite historical conditions but a permanent possibility of *Dasein*: it is always open to us to pursue either the 'authentic' or the 'inauthentic' mode of being. But if 'inauthenticity' belongs to the fundamental structure of human being, then escape from it would seem to be entirely a matter of individual 'enlightenment' and to require no transformation in the state of the world as a whole. And Heidegger was, in fact, persuaded that it was only through the temporary emergence from 'inauthenticity' of privileged individuals that any historical progress could come about. The rest of the human race were condemned to the 'inauthenticity' of mediocre 'average-ness' and their behaviour in that sense amenable to positivist understanding.

In defending his position, Heidegger argues that to treat 'reification'[5] as affecting a subject only in specific historical conditions is to presume to know what is 'truly human' – to presuppose that we have knowledge of Being (including the Being of *Dasein* as part of it) – when it is precisely that which must be the prior object of investigation. It was on these same grounds that he rejected every traditional humanist theory (including that of Marx – of whom he reveals, however, a very minimal knowledge). In his 'Letter on Humanism', Heidegger argues that since traditional humanist argument precedes from 'an already established interpretation of nature, history, world and the ground of the world . . . of beings as a whole', it is ontologically committed to defining humanity by reference to, or in contrast with, the 'animal' and the 'natural'. Such definitions, he suggests, are 'metaphysical' evasions.

Are we really on the right track towards the essence of man as long as we set him off as one living creature amongst others in contrast to plants, beasts and God? We can proceed in that way; we can in such fashion locate man within being as one being amongst others. We will thereby be able to state something correct about man. But we must be clear on this point, that when we do this we abandon man to the essential realm of *animalitas* but attribute a specific difference to him. In principle we are still thinking of *homo animalis* – even when *anima* (soul) is posited as *animus sive mens* (spirit or mind), and this in turn is later posited as subject, person, or spirit (*geist*). Such positing is the manner of metaphysics. But the essence of man is too little heeded and not thought in its origin, the essential provenance that is always the essential future for historical mankind. Metaphysics thinks on the basis of *animalitas* and does not think in the direction of his *humanitas* (p. 202).[6]

According to Heidegger, therefore, naturalistic definitions of humanity completely fail to capture its essence, because like all traditional metaphysical definitions they naïvely assume that we know what we mean when we say of something that 'it is', or ascribe 'being' to it. Hence Heidegger not only questions the propriety of calling his own thought a 'humanism' ('should we still keep the name "humanism"', he asks, 'for a "humanism" that contradicts all previous humanism – though it in no way advocates the inhuman?'), but also rejects the term 'existentialist' as interpreted by Sartre, arguing that metaphysics is not overthrown simply by reversing its 'basic tenet' that essence precedes existence (p. 204). Even existentialism fails to face the question of Being, since it does not understand that the metaphysical categories of 'essentia' and 'existentia' must be dismantled *before* any statement can be made about the relation between them. The implication of this critique of metaphysics is that:

the highest determinations of the essence of man in humanism still do not realise the proper dignity of man. To that extent the thinking in *Being and Time* is against humanism. But this opposition does not mean that such thinking aligns itself against the humane and advocates the inhuman, that it promotes the inhumane and deprecates the dignity of man. Humanism is opposed because it does not set the *humanitas* of man high enough (p. 208).

But how are we to recognize the proper dignity of humanity? Not, according to Heidegger, by making man the 'Subject' or sovereign centre of beings – 'so that as the tyrant of Being he may deign to release the beingness of beings into an all too loudly bruited "objectivity"' (p. 210) – but by acknowledging that the destiny of man is to *ek-sist*, which implies being more than 'merely human', more than a mere 'rational creature':

Man is not the lord of beings. Man is the shepherd of being. Man loses nothing in this 'less'; rather he gains in that he attains the truth of Being. He gains the essential poverty of the shepherd, whose dignity consists in his being called by Being itself into the preservation of Being's truth (p. 221).

The realization of this pastoral vocation (for which, as we have seen, Heidegger believes that few are chosen) requires the rejection of 'subjectivizing' thought. Subjectivizing thought refuses simply to let things be, insisting instead upon evaluating them from the standpoint of the subject; it 'lets being be valid solely as the objects of its doing' (p. 228). Yet Heidegger also maintains, problematically, that 'to think against values . . . is not to beat the drum for the valuelessness and nullity of beings'. It means rather 'to bring the lighting of the truth of Being before thinking, as against subjectivizing beings into mere objects' (p. 228).

The 'shepherding of being' is presented as contemplative. Heidegger rejects the arrogant anthropocentricity of the positivist attitude, arguing that we must think against the values imposed by the 'fact–value' distinction; and he insists that we have fallen into 'inauthenticity' through an excess of theory and interpretation. But his only remedy is the adoption of the meditative attitude which will 'illuminate Being' through merely 'letting it be'. Heidegger claims to propound an ethics, but we may well ask how far this is consistent with the instruction to think 'against values'. We may also feel that Heidegger has himself succumbed to 'metaphysical' definitions and evaluations of humanity when he insists that it is mankind's 'essential dignity' and 'Being' that is betrayed by all traditional humanist thought.

Jean-Paul Sartre and existentialism

Despite the ambivalence of Heidegger's 'existentialism', it was his fidelity to the original 'existentialist' programme of Husserlian phenomenology – namely, the exploration of 'being-in-the-world' rather than of the structures of consciousness – that recommended his philosophy to Sartre. Sartre argued, however, that Heidegger had liberated philosophy from the transcendental ego only at the cost of disallowing any appeal to consciousness in the description of *Dasein*. His aim, therefore, in *Being and Nothingness* was to accommodate the intentional role of consciousness without reverting to subjective idealism. By integrating Husserl and Heidegger in a manner that would allow the one to correct the other, he hoped to provide an account of intentional consciousness in-the-world as it is lived.

What underlay this project was a belief in the total and unqualified nature of human freedom. Husserl's notion of a structured consciousness had, therefore, to be discarded, since if thought was structured it was also regulated. At the same time, Sartre rejected Heidegger's undifferentiated ontological monism on the grounds that it made it impossible for consciousness (the 'for-itself') to encounter anything radically different from consciousness (pure 'thinghood', 'the in-itself'). In taking Being to be always already 'for humanity', Heidegger left the individual with no freedom to construct meaning – to 'choose' a personal way of being in the world.

Sartre insists, by contrast, on the dualism of Being and Consciousness (Nothingness). On the one hand there is the uninterpreted, eternal, uncreated 'thingness' of the world, on the other, consciousness as nothingness – as pure outwardness to the objectivity of the world in which it is situated. If we treat this doctrine as Sartre intended – as an attempt to provide a metaphysical foundation for human freedom – it hardly seems tenable. For how are we to make sense of a consciousness that is a nothingness 'acting upon' the 'in-itself'? Inversely, if no actual state of the world can provide the motive for action, how *are* we to account for our conscious projects? The doctrine is no more satisfactory from an ethical and political point of view, since the dualism of for-itself and in-itself, which is supposed to guarantee the absoluteness of freedom, and to provide the basis of human choice and responsibility, actually works in the reverse direction, undermining the very possibility of freedom it is designed to preserve. As many critics of *Being and Nothingness* have noted, Sartre's theory of the absoluteness of human freedom obliterates ordinary distinctions between 'voluntary' and 'involuntary' action, and therefore belittles the status of those limited but concrete freedoms which we aspire to protect and enlarge. The choice between slave or master, exploited or exploiter, is not the matter of indifference which Sartre implies when he argues that ultimately it is we who 'choose' every state of our being. When indeed he writes in *Being and Nothingness* that it is 'I who decide the coefficient of adversity in things and even their unpredictability' then it is not so much freedom that is advocated but an infinite capacity to adapt to all situations.

Moreover, while Sartre stresses the responsibility imposed by total freedom, he could equally well have emphasized the inconsequentiality of making decisions. For if we freely choose whatever adversity we encounter, then have we any more reason to alter it than to accept it? Can we, indeed, act effectively to 'change' a world construed as amenable to any construction we put upon it? Freely though perpetually 'anguished' by a choice we have to make, oppressed by the very freedom that we cannot but submit to, we are what we are, we do what we do – and that is all that can be said. Such argument, however, ignores the extent to which human beings *cannot* adapt and remain alive and/or sane; it also detracts from the rationality of their refusal to do so.

Simone de Beauvoir

As early as 1949 Simone de Beauvoir had drawn attention to the complication which the oppression of women represents for any theory of absolute freedom. In *The Second Sex*, the categories of 'project', 'freedom' and 'transcendence' are used to argue that to be a woman, as distinct from a man, is to be Other, both to oneself and to others:

> Every individual concerned to justify his existence feels that his existence involves an undefined need to transcend himself, to engage in freely chosen projects . . . what peculiarly signalizes the situation of women is that she – a free and autonomous being like all human creatures – nevertheless finds herself in a world where men compel her to assume the status of Other. They propose to stabilize her as object and doom her to immanence since her transcendence is to be overshadowed and for ever transcended by another ego (*conscience*) which is essential and sovereign.[7]

De Beauvoir also challenges Sartre's portrayal in *Being and Nothingness* of the female body as a threat to male subjecthood, which deprives women themselves of any final transcendence.[8] For she stresses that what she aspires to is not the pre-eminence of women over men, nor the mere switching of the roles played by 'man' and 'woman' in the Sartrean struggle for transcendence, but reciprocity between the sexes. 'To emancipate woman', she claims in the final lines of the book, 'is to refuse to confine her to the relations she bears to man, not to deny them to her; let her have her independent existence and she will continue nonetheless to exist for him *also*.'

Consistent with her commitment to the essential tenets of existentialism, de Beauvoir maintains that women, though robbed of their subjectivity, are no less existentially free than men, and that it is therefore women's existence as human beings rather than as females which must provide the basis of every feminist demand. Women, in short, are human first and women second. This rules out both reactionary justifications for their subordination on the grounds of their natural inferiority or distinctive sexuality (hence her quarrel with biologism and a good deal of Freudianism); but it also rules out more positive 'feminist' demands for a recognition of some specifically feminine essence.

It is an argument, however, that is not always easily reconciled with some of its Hegelian and Sartrean packaging. The main problem is the extent to which *The Second Sex* endorses the view of our relations with others that Sartre derives from Hegel's Master–Slave dialectic. For the moral that Sartre draws from the Hegelian story is (contrary to Hegel) that the Master alone is truly free (since not dependent upon any determinate mode of existence), and that we are doomed to permanent conflict in our relations with others. Hegel is wrong, according to Sartre, to suppose that consciousness can present itself as an object to itself, through the mediation of the Other, without thereby ceasing to be self-aware. To retain one's subjecthood is necessarily to objectify the Other (who must cease at that point to reflect one's selfhood), and vice versa.[9] 'So long as consciousnesses exist', says Sartre, 'the separation and conflict of consciousness will remain. . . .'[10] It is this reformulation of the Master–Slave dialectic which de Beauvoir herself appears to accept when she speaks of the 'fundamental hostility' of consciousnesses to each other.[11] And to the extent that this mutual hostility between persons is mapped, in her account, on to relations between the sexes, it would seem to render the sexual reciprocity for which she calls impossible. For it would imply that while it is a contingent and historical truth that men gained the upper hand in the struggle for subjectivity, the struggle itself, along with the objectification of the Other that is the condition of victory in it, must remain an essential framework. That in turn implies that the most we can hope for in the way of equality between the sexes is parity between antagonists.

Nor is it entirely clear, in fact, that de Beauvoir does not herself reproduce a certain contempt for everything 'feminine' in her injunction to women to realize themselves in a *transcendence* of their existence as Otherness – for it is a demand that implicitly accepts the conception of the female body as an obstacle to freedom. As Genevieve Lloyd has pointed out, 'transcendence' is in its origins, a transcendence *of* the feminine: in the Hegelian version, it is a transcendence of the 'nether world' of women; in the Sartrean, a repudiation of the female body and its threat to subjectivity. Hence, she concludes, it is perhaps hardly surprising if women are viewed by de Beauvoir as capable of 'transcendence' only at the expense of alienation from their bodily being.[12]

None the less, *The Second Sex* remains the most substantial philosophical discussion of the condition of women yet produced, and its exposure of the masculinism implicit in a great deal of existentialist humanism is of permanent importance.

Maurice Merleau-Ponty

Merleau-Ponty's celebrated criticism of *Being and Nothingness* for remaining a philosophy of consciousness – for being '*at* the world but not *in* it' – is usually associated with his own rejection of a 'Cartesian' dualism between consciousness and world. It is more seldom noted that this criticism was made against Sartre in the light of an intuitive, and indeed partially theorized, understanding of the relations between Marxism and existentialism for which Sartre himself was to argue fifteen years later. In an essay written in 1948, Merleau-Ponty writes that

> The dialectic between being and nothingness takes place not only in Sartre's mind but also in the mind of the down-hearted worker who is withdrawing from the struggle. Who would dare insist that no condemned man feel anguish at his death, even if he dies for his class and, through it, for the future of mankind? As soon as man is introduced as the subject of history – and Marxism so portrays him – one is no longer bringing in merely collective man or class but is also including individual man who retains his power to serve or to betray his class and who in this sense joins it for his own accord. Marx gives us an objective definition of class in terms of the effective position of individuals in the production cycle, but he tells us elsewhere that class cannot become a decisive historical force and revolutionary factor unless individuals become aware of it, adding that this awareness itself has social motives, and so on. As a historical factor, class is therefore neither a simple objective fact, nor is it, on the other hand, a simple value arbitrarily chosen by solitary

consciousnesses. It is more in the nature of a fact-value or an incarnate value, for which the theory remains to be worked out.[13]

In another essay of the same period, to be found in *Sense and Non-Sense*, he writes that 'economic life is not a separate order to which other orders may be reduced; it is Marxism's way of representing the inertia of human life' (p. 108). Or again, rejecting the notion of a transindividual subject of history or guiding economical rationality, while recognizing the counter-finality or, as Sartre was later to term it, 'primary alienation' to which collective human action is liable, he writes that

the logic of history does not operate in terms of clear ideas and individual projects; its instruments are the complex politics and anonymous projects which give a group of individuals a certain common style, 'fascist', for example, or 'proletarian'. In so far as we have not understood that our actions take on a certain statistical and objective meaning (which may be quite different from that which we give them) when they pass from us into things, we are surprised by them, do not recognize them, and are misled by the 'mysterious power of autodetermination' with which . . . history seems endowed (p. 111).

Though Merleau-Ponty was later to abandon Marxism, his sense of history's 'ambiguous' logic and his notion of 'incarnate value' remain keys to the comprehension of his later work. History, according to Merleau-Ponty, is both contingent and rational. There are true doctrines, he argues, which do not get written into history, and, inversely, there are conspicuous events which do not carry history forward. Yet there is a rationality in history in so far as it presents us with effective problems demanding solution if we are to escape barbarism, or to prosper at all. Moreover, there are only certain forces and movements at any time that are capable of guiding history to its rational destination, and it is for these that individuals must assume responsibility. There is no guarantee that the 'truth' of history (which Merleau-Ponty then thought to be embodied in the proletarian movement for socialism) will be adopted as a conscious project, nor is there any assurance that those projects which are willed will be successful. But if we give ourselves to it, history will itself respond: 'politics . . . is not created *ex nihilo* in the minds of individuals but is prepared and worked out in history', for history itself 'contains vectors; it has a meaning – not that all things falls into place in terms of one end, but because it rejects the men and the institutions which do not respond to existing problems . . .' (p. 105). To stay in touch with existing problems is to bring truth or meaning into history by assuming responsibility for it.

It was Merleau-Ponty's conviction of the 'open-endedness' of history and of the need for philosophy to register the simultaneously 'contingent' (and hence 'free') and 'situated' (and hence 'conditioned') quality of human being, that determined his attitude to the two thinkers by whom he was most influenced, Hegel and Husserl.

Applauding Hegel for his 'attempt to explore the irrational and to integrate it into an expanded reason', Merleau-Ponty sees in him the 'inventor' of a Reason 'broader than the understanding, which can repeat the variety and singularity of individual consciousnesses, civilisations, ways of thinking and historical contingency, but which nevertheless does not give up the attempt to master them in order to guide them to their truth' (p. 63). He argues, none the less, that Hegel failed to sustain this dialectic of individual and historical consciousness since he ended by allowing the absorption of human subjectivity within the idealist dream of an end of history, the dialectic and all contradiction. Hegel denied the contingency of history, and thus the role of human individuals in its making; instead of preserving the freedom of humanity, he subordinated individuals to historical necessity.

Merleau-Ponty also argues that despite Kojève's efforts to interpret Hegel as a precursor of Husserl, what is markedly absent from Hegel's 'phenomenology' is a sense of the relativity of its own philosophy: by reserving to himself the perch of 'absolute knowledge' from which to chart the progress of the Idea, Hegel conceals the situatedness of his own philosophy within the historical process he aims to record.

While appearing at times to regard Hegel's idealism as an aberration rather than an inevitable outcome of his philosophy, Merleau-Ponty in fact viewed its dualist ontology of consciousness and world as fundamentally flawed. On this same ground he criticized both Husserl's concept of the transcendental ego and Sartre's account of consciousness in *Being and Nothingness*. But if Merleau-Ponty rejected the idea of a 'pure thought' – of a consciousness prior to the world and to language – it was because he acknowledged how difficult it was to provide a dialectical account of the subject, not because he thought the attempt to do so should be abandoned in principle. Merleau-Ponty's philosophy supports neither the eradication of the subject nor the reduction of the world to textuality.

For him, the acquisition of language is certainly a precondition of thought, and in that sense precedes it, there being no way in which the subject can confer meaning upon signs that are devoid of it. Yet the subject remains at the origin of every expression, and it is only by reference to the speaker that we can hope to specify why *this* is said, not *that*. At the same time, language itself is only possible because there exists an extra-linguistic grounding for it in the world.[14] There is no communication that is not relative to culture and language; yet what underlies this relativity is the ineffable absoluteness of the world 'as such'. Prior to any language, this 'primordial layer' of being underlies the humanity–nature, subject–object dichotomies that are fundamental to Hegelian and Sartrean dialectics.

Given this acceptance of a preconscious level of being, by which subjective consciousness is itself conditioned, one might hesitate to refer to Merleau-Ponty's philosophy as 'humanist'. Yet the human subject is always, for Merleau-Ponty, a point of origin, from which we have to begin if we would understand history, and to which we must always refer in the explanation of language or any other signifying system. And if this is the case, it is by virtue of the 'contingency' which radically distinguishes *human* being from the rest of nature. In the final analysis, Merleau-Ponty remains faithful to the fundamental thesis of existentialist humanism, there being, according to him, no essence predetermining human existence: 'Man' brings his being into being, both actually as a natural subject who works on the basis of consciously chosen projects to create a world, and epistemologically – as the privileged 'knower' of the world and bringer of meaning to it.

Jean-Paul Sartre and Marxism

Within a year of publication of his philosophical analysis of the 'uselessness' of human passion, and of the necessary conflict to which we are doomed in our relations with others, Sartre was defiantly proclaiming that 'existentialism is no mournful delectation, but a humanist philosophy of action, effort, combat and solidarity.[15] A shift in perspective away from the nihilism of *Being and Nothingness* is also noticeable in Sartre's 'Presentation' of *Les Temps Modernes* which he founded with Merleau-Ponty in 1946 and where he argues with eloquence and vigour for the necessity of the writer's political commitment. It is only, however, in *What is Literature?* (1948) that this shift finds a reflection in theory.[16] In this text, the author–reader community is presented as the way out of the 'humanist' dilemma between being for oneself and being for others. Through art, and particularly in the act of reading, according to Sartre, we are able finally to recognize ourselves in an object that does not objectify us in the sense of treating us as 'mere object'. For the author, too, the ontological conflict of subjectivity–objectivity is overcome: as a free creation undetermined by any prior purpose or instrumentality, the work of art provides the 'sole case in which the creator gets any enjoyment out of the subject he creates'.[17] The aesthetic dimension thus comes to be viewed by Sartre as evoking a free community of equals prefiguring the possible transcendence of a conflict which in *Being and Nothingness* is ascribed to the human condition as such. Through reading and writing as a synthesized act of 'confidence in the freedom of men', Sartre argues that the Kantian Kingdom of Ends is realized by thousands of readers all over the world who do not know each other. The aspiration to experience genuinely free relations is not doomed to frustration, but represents a real historical possibility of socialism intimated in the 'imaginary' world of art.[18]

But if Sartre begins to cut himself free of the ontology of *Being and Nothingness* in *What is Literature?*, it is only in the *Critique of Dialectical Reason* (1960) that he is fully prepared to recognize the concrete, material constraints upon the exercise of freedom. In the *Critique*, in fact, Sartre allows that our freedom is limited in two important respects, one necessary, the other contingent. In the first place, he acknowledges the truth of the claim made by Marx and Engels in *The German Ideology* that we are creatures of need, who must eat, drink, house and clothe ourselves, etc. as a condition of doing anything else. All human *praxis*, says Sartre, must therefore be understood as an attempt to negate need. (The terminology of negation rather than of 'satisfaction' is expressive of Sartre's general attitude to human purpose. As we might expect of the author of *Being and Nothingness*, the emphasis falls on the annihilation of lack rather than upon the intrinsic pleasure of action and consumption.)[19] Second, the struggle against need is conditioned by the fact that it takes place – and will continue to do so for the foreseeable future – in conditions of scarcity. This results in competition for resources, exploitation of some by others, and the constant possibility that one individual's freedom may limit another's. In the relations of 'alterity' that derive from scarcity, each individual experiences the other as 'one too many' – as a threat to his or her own survival and continued *praxis*.

The necessity imposed by scarcity is revealed to dialectical understanding as a 'strictly foreseeable and utterly unforeseen alteration' of each individual's objectified *praxis* by the *praxis* of every other; its concrete outcome is the 'practico-inert' – Sartre's term for the congealed and reified product of concerted but non-unified human activity. In the *Critique*, then, Sartre recognizes that there are both natural and humanly contrived constraints upon the exercise of an unbridled freedom. None the less, the *necessity* of the practico-inert lies, precisely, in its being a humanly created passivity. The factory worker, Sartre concedes, cannot choose but comply with the rhythm of the machine she operates; and yet she is dominated by the machine only to the extent that things themselves become the relays of human action. Behind the machine, and the assembly line, there is a multiplicity of workers brought together through the pseudo-unity of the factory and linked by a destiny which must be undergone in common. Freedom here no longer means the possibility of choice but the necessity of taking some action in response to any set of circumstances in which we happen to find ourselves. We are conditioned by each situation, but each situation is itself compounded by actions taken in reaction to it. In this sense, the 'incapacity' to do otherwise than comply with a given situation is made accountable to a regressive accumulation of responses to the demand that 'we do something'. What conditions us is not purely material: it is the practico-inert, a complex synthesis of human materiality. An impersonal and 'serial' multiplicity of choices replaces the personal choice theorized in *Being and Nothingness*, but individual *praxis* remains the basis of all human history. It is such *praxis* which brought into being the alienation of the factory (of the labour camp, of the world market, of the nuclear arsenal . . .) and it is therefore only concerted individual *praxes* that can release the hold of these monstrous 'relays' of human intentionality.

Though Sartre presents alienation as rooted in scarcity, rather than in the division of labour, and regards the overthrow of capitalism as insufficient for its removal, the logic of his argument is the same as that which guides the discussion of alienation in *The German Ideology*: Sartre respects – as he illuminates – the Marxist account of individuals as both 'subjects' and 'objects' of history (see pp. 38–40 above). At the same time, he insists that history is only intelligible because it is dialectical, because, that is, it records a process brought into being by human action. To postulate a dialectic of nature, he argues, would be to suppose that human history is simply a variant of natural history. Those Marxists who do indeed claim to know the truth of history on the basis of a 'dialectics of nature' have simply opted for dogmatism (the converse of scepticism). Such Marxists can only 'justify' the claim to scientificity by endorsing positivism. They must argue, that is, that an 'objective' sociology is possible. As a phenomenologist, however, Sartre rejects as profoundly erroneous the idea that there could be an 'objective' supra- or trans-individual 'knowledge' of humanity: if history is to be intelligible, it must be intelligible in terms of the individuals whose actions compound it. 'However one looks at it,' he writes, 'transcendental materialism leads to the irrational, *either* by ignoring the thought of empirical man, *or* by creating a noumenal consciousness which imposes its law as a whim, *or again*, by discovering in Nature "*without* alien addition" the laws of dialectical Reason in the form of contingent facts.'[20] If there is no trans-individual comprehension, then there can be no trans-individual subject. History is neither a 'process without a subject' nor the product of a 'collective personage' or hyper-individual. Sartre, however, by no means supposes that individuals can be understood without appreciation of the formative role of social mediations in their constitution, or that they act as wholly independent units in the making of history. He certainly recognizes that the ensembles or structures which dominate human action lack a subject in the sense that their meaning is not reducible to any particular individual design;[21] and in an attempt to comprehend the possibility of emancipation from the dominance of circumstance, he distinguishes between the 'constituent' dialectic of individual *praxis* and the 'constituted' dialectic of group action.

Sartre describes as 'serial' those impersonal and essentially fragmented processes whereby individuals are related socially but anonymously – the unity of a serial nexus is always unlocatably 'somewhere else'. Such processes – which have all the appearance of being regulated by synthesizing forces, but are not consciously organized or in any sense deliberately orchestrated – occur at all levels of social complexity, and can be more or less permanent features of it. Bus queues or movements of fashions are serial; so, too, are the mechanisms of price formation on the market, or social classes or religious followings in so far as these exist merely as passive multiplicities of persons.

In contrast to such unauthored and uncoordinated processes the 'group' fuses individuals in a single *praxis* common to them all and accountable to each. Sartre's main example is the transformation of a dispersed and 'serial' resentment into the 'general will' which stormed the Bastille in 1789. With the formation of the 'fused group', solitude as the defining characteristic of the series (it is both the absence of the link between its individuals and the link itself in that it specifies the interchangeability of elements in an open-ended system) gives way to synthetic unity. In order to explain how this comes about, Sartre introduces the notion of the 'third party' who totalizes the situation of two solitary persons (the dyad) but in doing so recognizes her or his involvement in the totality so constituted. Each member of a group is a 'third party' in this way and the group itself is thus constituted by means of a double mediation of the group between 'third parties' and of each 'third party' between the group and other 'third parties'.

Group *praxis* is to be understood in the first instance in terms of survival: the group acts to overcome the threat which motivated its original fusion. With the passing of the immediate threat, the action for survival cedes to that of the pledge – a freely made decision on the part of each member to remain loyal to the group. Both actions are generated by fear, but in the case of the pledge it is no longer of an 'external' enemy; it is inspired by the internal *praxis* of the group as such: it is fear of the penalty to be paid for defection.

Within this framework, Sartre seeks to analyse group organization, function, structure and process with the overall aim of discovering how a group can both negate individual *praxis*, and yet be able to pursue its communal ends as goals freely adopted by the individuals who pledge themselves to it. The Sartrean 'fused group' is both an ideal of democratic practice, and that which makes the possibility of any such practice intelligible.

Since the group has no reality apart from the *praxes* which comprise it, its unity is essentially practical rather than ontological. It is none the less in the nature of the group that it seeks to attain an ontological stability, and this inevitability leads to its institutionalization. It attempts to guarantee its continued existence by the introduction of legislation and sanctions which secure unity only at the cost of its lapse into seriality. Thereupon, a structure in which each individual *is* the function of unity is replaced by a structure in which each individual *performs* it – and thus becomes indefinitely replaceable.

The 'fused group' is therefore essentially unstable, a 'molten' entity constantly liable to cool into seriality. That it recongeals into a bureaucratic organization, or that its heady totalization of individual *praxes* becomes the warrant for the most totalitarian repression of individual freedom – these are the dangers that lie in wait for the 'group' the moment it attempts to capitalize upon the common inspiration that brought it into being by endowing it with more institutional form.

The dialectic of series and groups (which is the dialectic of history itself) is marked by a double circularity. On the one hand, there is the constant relatedness of group action to the series out of which it evolved; on the other hand, there is the constant movement from series to group and back. Sartre insists that this latter circularity, unlike the former, has no necessary sequence. History therefore, lacks any ultimate direction. The removal of the alienation of seriality through group action remains a permanent possibility, but its final abolition in the establishment of an authentic socialist community is in no sense guaranteed. Indeed, it is the message of the *Critique* that we cannot be both free *and* assured of emancipation. Socialism is not the inevitable destiny of the development of the productive forces; it is a value to be chosen, a goal to be adopted by a conscious human project of liberation.

The greatness of the *Critique* lies in the brilliance with which it captures an immediately recognizable but seldom articulated 'logic of progress' implicit in the formation of the party, or in the movement which leads from revolution into 'Stalinism', or in such social phenomena as bureaucracy, dictatorship, the cold war and the arms race. The *Critique* is also the first serious attempt by someone sympathetic to Marxism to spell out what is involved in the claim, set forth in the founding texts of historical materialism, that 'individuals make history'.

Many Marxists, of course, are dismissive of the *Critique* precisely because it 'starts from the individual', but this criticism is only telling for those who have already accepted, as a methodological principle that must guide all sociology, that 'societies' are logically prior to their individual members. If Sartre insists on the necessity of proceeding from individual *praxis*, it is because he is convinced that any other approach will result in reifying hypostatization of the social. It is important to understand that he analyses rather than presupposes the notion of the 'social'. The relevant contrast is not that of 'solitary' versus 'social' individual, but that of the 'plurality of individual activities' versus a 'hyper-individual Collectivity' or 'unitary' sociality.

As André Gorz has put it, in a defence of Sartre,

> If the individual is explicable through the society, but the society is not intelligible through individuals – that is, if the 'forces' that act in history are impermeable and radically heterogeneous to organic *praxis* – then socialism as the socialization of man can never coincide with socialism as the humanisation of the social. It cannot come from individuals as their reappropriation by collective *praxis* of the resultant of individual *praxes*. It can only come *to* individuals by the evolution of their society according to its inner logic . . .

and hence only by a 'submission of individuals to society and its demands on them', rather than by a 'submission of society and history to individuals and their demands'.[22] Here, the distinction is between capitalism as the alienated product of collective or plural activities whose sociality is manifested only in 'serial' form, and socialism as sociality 'conscious of itself', as collective activity unified by a common aim. Neither Sartre nor Gorz is arguing that pre-socialist society is comprised of 'pre-social' individuals, as Ronald Aronson appears to suppose when, rejecting (and significantly misquoting) Gorz's argument, he writes that

> socialism makes no sense as the 'reappropriation by collective *praxis* of the resultant of individual *praxis*', but only as the reappropriation of the resultant of heretofore alienated collective *praxis* . . . we can restore the intellectual possibility of human beings making history and controlling their society, without basing their social life on imaginary pre-social individuals.[23]

Aronson has rather more basis for his quarrel with Sartre's account of scarcity, given that this is presented, if not as an ontological condition of humanity, as none the less the context of all human production now and in the foreseeable future. For while it is true that certain (though by no means all) natural resources are scarce in the sense that they are finite and non-reproducible, this indicates the need for global consumption to remain within their limits – limits which could, in fact, permit a very decent if not overly luxurious standard of living for all the inhabitants of the globe today. Given that all the most disastrous scarcities of our times are accountable to the extraordinary *affluence* of the industrialized nations of the world, there is something profoundly misleading in Sartre's supposition that lack is fundamental to human society today. No argument is acceptable which implies that 'nature' is in some way to blame for dearth; nor can we allow that a problem caused by grotesque exploitation should be presented as if it were soluble only through increased technical mastery over nature. The 'scarcity' of oil, for example, could be overcome if we ceased to rely so extensively on private cars; food would cease to be scarce if Third World countries were no longer obliged to grow cash crops for export in order to meet their 'debts' to the First World; medicine and schooling will become less 'scarce' when armaments became more so, and so on. It is therefore quite inappropriate to conceptualize scarcity as a kind of absolute or permanent feature of existence that is merely 'displaced' from one area to another while remaining itself intact.[24] For we are condemned to scarcity only pending a political agreement to revolutionize our structures of production and consumption. In this sense, there is no 'basic' scarcity at the root of alienation, and to suppose that there is, is to accept too unquestioningly the 'necessity' of contemporary patterns of consumption.

What unbalances the *Critique* is the conflictual model of relations between humanity and nature that underlies it. Sartre assumes (and it is an assumption which stems from and reinforces his ontological dualism) that the natural world is not only *other*, but also hostile. It is this conception of nature as the 'enemy' that accounts for the presentation of a 'natural' scarcity as responsible for relations of alterity; and it also underlies his account of 'primary alienation' – of an alienation attributable to the stubbornly resistant 'otherness' of materiality as such.

Such a viewpoint, however, not only reproduces the imperialism of much classical humanism (which sees nature as an alien in need of civilization rather than an ally we may need ourselves to learn to emulate in certain respects); it also conflicts with a vision of a socialist future based on a harmonization of human needs with those of ecology, and it encourages the view that human relations, together with the institutions and structures they generate, must be seen as oppressive. Power itself, in Sartre's understanding of things, tends to be presented as violence, and the possibility that it can operate positively in the interests of both humanity and nature conjointly (and that, indeed, it must so operate if the world is to survive at all), is therefore overlooked.

Notes

1. Edmund Husserl, *The Crisis of European Sciences and Transcendental Phenomenology*, trans. by David Carr (Evanston 1970), pp. 123-35.
2. Husserl, *The Crisis of European Sciences*, p. 15.
3. ibid.
4. On the similarities between Heidegger and Lukács, see Lucien Goldmann, *Lukács and Heidegger*, trans. William Q. Boelhower (London 1977), pp. 14-24.
5. Lucien Goldmann claims (*Lukács and Heidegger*, p. 17) that it is almost certain that the discussion of 'reification' in *Being and Time* is directed against Lukács even though Heidegger never mentions him by name.
6. Page numbers here and in the text following refer to Martin Heidegger, 'Letter on Humanism', in *Basic Writings* (London 1977). The *Letter* was in part occasioned by the publication of Sartre's *Existentialism is a Humanism* (first published Paris 1946).
7. Simone de Beauvoir, *The Second Sex*, trans. H. M. Parshley (Harmondsworth 1972), p. 29.
8. Jean-Paul Sartre, *Being and Nothingness*, trans. Hazel Barnes (London 1958), part IV, ch. 2, section 3. Sartre's sexism is roundly condemned in M. Collins and C. Pierce, 'Holes and Slime: Sexism in Sartre's Psychoanalysis', in C. Gould and M. Wartofsky (eds), *Women and Philosophy* (New York 1980), pp. 112-27 and is a target of attack of many feminists.
9. Sartre, *Being and Nothingness*, p. 242f.; see Genevieve Lloyd's discussion in 'Masters, Slaves and Others', *Radical Philosophy*, no. 34 (summer 1983), esp. p. 6; see also her *The Man of Reason* (London 1984).
10. Sartre, *Being and Nothingness*, pp. 214 and 244.
11. de Beauvoir, *The Second Sex*, p. 17.
12. Genevieve Lloyd, 'Masters, Slaves and others', pp. 7-9.
13. Maurice Merleau-Ponty, 'The Battle over Existentialism' in *Sense and Non-Sense*, trans. Hubert L. Dreyfus and Patricia Allen Dreyfus (Evanston 1964), p. 80. Ensuing page numbers in the text refer to this work.
14. See the discussion in Maurice Merleau-Ponty, *The Visible and the Invisible* (Evanston 1968), esp. pp. 180-200; also Cornelius Castoriadis, *The Crossroads in the Labyrinth* (Brighton 1984), pp. 119-44.

15 '*A propos de l'existentialisme: mise au point*', *Action* (29 December, 1944).
16 Ronald Aronson, *Jean-Paul Sartre, Philosophy in the World* (London 1980), p. 121.
17 *What is Literature?*, trans. Bernard Frechtman (New York 1948), p. 39.
18 ibid., pp. 32-57 and 264-5.
19 See Jonathan Rée, 'Half a Critique', *Radical Philosophy*, no. 15 (autumn 1976), who writes that in eliding the form and the content of *praxis*, Sartre rules out 'the possibility that, say, the water and the sunshine, the wine and the conversation, could simply be enjoyed because – for some contingent reason and as a matter of brute fact – they satisfy your needs and desires . . .'.
20 Jean-Paul Sartre, *Critique of Dialectical Reason*, trans. A. Sheridan-Smith, ed. Jonathan Rée (London 1976), p. 32.
21 Sartre is by no means unique in doing so. Many would insist that it is precisely this view of historical process that is upheld by Marx and Engels themselves, while Vico and William Morris were certainly proponents of it. See also E. P. Thompson's discussion of Vico, Engels and Morris as sharing a common understanding of history as a process ensuing 'in regularities which do not conform to the actors' intentions', *The Poverty of Theory* (London 1978), pp. 276-81.
22 André Gorz, 'Sartre and Marx', in *Western Marxism, a Critical Reader* (London 1977), p. 182.
23 Ronald Aronson, 'The Individualist Social Theory of Jean-Paul Sartre', in Gorz, *Western Marxism*, pp. 225-6.
24 Expounding Sartre's argument, Gorz writes (*Western Marxism*, p. 192): 'every *local* and partial victory over scarcity brings with it a *displacement* of scarcity into other areas . . .'.

Further reading

The main source texts for the argument discussed in this chapter are: Edmund Husserl, *Ideas* (1913), trans. W. R. Boyce Gibson (London 1931); *The Crisis of European Sciences and Transcendental Philosophy* (1954), trans. David Carr (Evanston 1970); Martin Heidegger, *Being and Time* (1926), trans. John Macquarrie and Edward Robinson (New York 1962); 'Letter on Humanism', in *Basic Writings*, ed. David Farrell Krell (London 1977). See also *The Question Concerning Technology and Other Essays*, trans. William Lovitt (New York 1976); *Introduction to Metaphysics*, trans. Ralph

Mannheim (New Haven 1959); Jean-Paul Sartre, *Being and Nothingness* (1943), trans. Hazel Barnes (London 1958); *What is Literature?* (1948), trans. Bernard Frechtman (New York 1948); *Existentialism and Humanism* (1946), trans. P. Mairet (London 1948); *Critique of Dialectical Reason* (1960), trans. A. Sheridan-Smith, ed. Jonathan Rée (London 1976). Maurice Merleau-Ponty, *Phenomenology of Perception* (1945), trans. Colin Smith (New York 1962); *Structure of Behaviour* (1942), trans. A. L. Fisher (Boston 1963); *The Primacy of Perception* (Evanston 1964) (a collection of studies written 1947–61); *Sense and Non-Sense* (1948), trans. Hubert L. Dreyfus and Patricia A. Dreyfus (Northwestern 1964); *Signs* (part III) (1960), trans. Richard C. McCleary (Evanston 1964); Simone de Beauvoir, *The Second Sex* (1949), trans. H. M. Parshley (Harmondsworth 1972).

A useful introduction to Husserl and bibliographical guide to phenomenology is provided by Roger Waterhouse, 'Husserl and Phenomenology', *Radical Philosophy*, no. 16 (spring 1977). A survey of interpretations of Heidegger's 'Letter on Humanism' is to be found in Robert Henri Cousineau, *Humanism and Ethics: An Introduction to Heideggers 'Letter on Humanism'* (Paris 1982). Helpful introductions to Heidegger's work as a whole are provided by Walter Biemel, *Martin Heidegger: an illustrated study*, trans. J. L. Mehta (London 1978), and Roger Waterhouse.

Sartre's objections to Husserl's account of consciousness are set forth in *The Transcendence of the Ego* (1937), trans. and intro. Forrest Williams and Robert Kirkpatrick (London 1957) (see especially, part I). Sartre's debt to Husserl and Heidegger is discussed by Ronald Aronson, *Jean-Paul Sartre, Philosophy in the World* (London 1980), pp. 91–6, and see also Istvan Meszaros, *The Work of Sartre*, vol. I: *Search for Freedom* (Brighton 1979), ch. 4.

For criticism of the existentialist reading of Hegel, Husserl and Heidegger, see Jacques Derrida, 'The Ends of Man', *Philosophical and Phenomenological Research*, **30** (1969), pp. 31–57 (now included in *Margins of Philosophy* (1972), trans. Alan Bates (Brighton 1982), pp. 119–54).

De Beauvoir's account of women is discussed by D. Kaufman McCall, 'Simone de Beauvoir, *The Second Sex* and Jean-Paul Sartre', *Signs*, **5** no. 2 (winter 1979); by Michele le Doeuff, 'Operative Philosophy: Simone de Beauvoir and existentialism', *Ideology and Consciousness*, **6** (autumn 1979); and by Genevieve Lloyd, *The Man of Reason* (London 1984) (who also provides further bibliography).

For an introduction to Merleau-Ponty's philosophy, see Sonia Kruks, *Radical Philosophy*, no. 11 (summer 1975). More extensive guidance is provided by Samuel B. Mallin, *Merleau-Ponty's Philosophy* (London 1979). See also, John F. Bannan, *The Philosophy of Merleau-Ponty* (New York 1967). A useful discussion and comparison of the philosophy and political attitudes of Sartre and Merleau-Ponty is to be found in: David Archard, *Marxism and Existentialism* (Blackstaff 1980); on Merleau-Ponty's points of contact with structuralist argument, see the article by John Mepham in David Robey (ed.), *Structuralism: an Introduction* (Oxford 1973).

General accounts of Sartre's career and philosophy are to be found in the works already cited by Aronson and Meszaros, which also discuss the more specific question of Sartre's Marxism. But see in addition: Jean-Paul Sartre, *Between Marxism and Existentialism* (1972), trans. John Mathews (London 1974); Pietro Chiodi, *Sartre and Marxism*, trans. Kate Soper (Hassocks 1975); the exchange between André Gorz and Ronald Aronson in *Western Marxism: A Critical Reader*, ed. New Left Review (London 1977); and Mark Poster, *Existential Marxism in Post-War France* (Princeton 1975).

Merleau-Ponty criticizes Sartre in the last part of his *Phenomenology of Perception*, and in 'Sartre and Ultra-Bolshevism' in *Adventures of the Dialectic* (1955), trans. Joseph Bien (Evanston 1973); see also *Humanism and Terror* (1946–7), trans. J. O'Neill (Evanston 1964).

For discussion of the influence of phenomenology on 'critical theory', see David Held, *Introduction to Critical Theory* (London 1980), ch. 5. See also, Theodor Adorno, 'Husserl and the Problem of Idealism', *Journal of Philosophy*, **XXVII** no. 1 (January 1940). Marcuse's pre-war attempt to combine Heideggerian and Marxist frameworks is discussed in Martin Jay, *The Dialectical Imagination* (London 1973), ch. 2; and see also Jay's recently published work, *Marxism and Totality* (Oxford 1984).

4
Humanism and political practice

Existentialism, cold war, and the question of 'engagement'

The 'existentialists' prided themselves on their insight into the 'situatedness' of their own thought, and related their theories explicitly to the political choices of the day. Moreover, in attributing historical outcomes to human *praxis*, they were at the same time implying that each of us has a responsibility to history. Hence their rejection of the idea that politics is the mere form of expression of impersonal contents, and the importance they attached to individual acts as irreducible determinants in themselves. Hence, too, their concern to provide a phenomenology of the 'lived experience' of political practice itself. In this sense, then, the historical and ideological context of the humanist argument in the post-war period is part of its intended content.

The framework of all political choice at the time was that provided by the rigid antitheses imposed by the cold war: West versus East, capitalism versus communism, NATO versus the Warsaw Pact. Such were the pressures exerted by this situation (which, of course, remains basically unchanged today) that the attempt to maintain a non-aligned politics was necessarily preoccupied with the essentially negative task of resisting misrepresentation and avoiding compromise.

The political difficulties of maintaining an independent stance in the cold war had their theoretical correlate in a hardening of the opposition between liberal and socialist thought – a process which has arguably left us with only perverted expressions of the original vision of both.

This is a schism, of course, which first came into being with the development of Marxist theory itself. By placing the class struggle on the political agenda Marx brought to an end an era in which political theorists, divided though they might have been on other issues were none the less able to appeal to a 'common interest' or 'general will'. Rousseau's vision of social harmony, Kant's invocation of the Kingdom of Ends, Hegel's ideas of the State as the manifestation of reason, or Mill's aspiration to combine participation of the masses with the privileging of the competent – all these came to seem anachronistic in the light of Marx's theory of history. Viewed from that perspective, appeals to a common humanity or to the harmonization of plural interests were to be seen as mystifying idealizations or even as direct apologies for the injustices perpetrated by the ruling class. At the same time, liberalism's 'humanist' defence of individual rights was no longer considered to be a sincere engagement with the perennial issue of individual freedom, but to be tainted from the outset by unconscious élitism and 'bourgeois' individualism.

There has also been a polarization within Marxist theory itself. This is attributable in part to the entrenchment of authoritarian socialist regimes in the East and the absence of socialist revolution in the West. In the West, Marxist thought has been carried into areas relatively neglected by Marx and Engels themselves, such as art and philosophy. 'Official' Marxism, however, has for long been identified with the mechanistic version of historical materialism formulated by Kautsky and Plekhanov in the Second International, reformulated by Bukharin in the Third, endorsed by Stalin and still adhered to in its essentials by the Communist Party of the Soviet Union.[1]

The initial political concern of the French existentialists was the development of a distinctively 'humanist' vision, rather than with the 'humanization' of Marxism itself. How, indeed, could political activity be reconciled with the existentialist ethic? Confronting this dilemma, Sartre insisted that the contradiction lay not in ideas

> but in my own being . . . for my liberty implied also the liberty of all men. And all men were not free. I could not submit to the discipline of solidarity with all men without breaking beneath the strain. And I could not be free alone.[2]

In a career in which this dilemma was never to be satisfactorily resolved, Sartre shifted from a position of initial political disengagement, through various degrees of commitment (though never membership) to the French Communist Party (*PCF*) to what has been called the 'unthinking activism'[3] of his final years. In this process, theory and practice were often at odds, and we encounter a continual dislocation between Sartre's activities as political *engagé*, novelist, dramatist and philosopher. Thus, when his political experience was forcing him to acknowledge a conflict between 'writing' and 'acting',[4] he was wishfully attempting to establish a creed of the writer's individual potency. Similarly when at work on *Being and Nothingness*, which many have regarded as philosophical legitimation of political apathy, he felt a need for commitment in his practical experience. Torn as he was between triumphant assertion of the power of the pen and acknowledgement of its impotence, between a scrupulous obedience to the necessity of discovering and communicating a meaning, and the purity of the immediate, spontaneous act, Sartre exemplified the frustrations to which any attempt by the individual to bridge the gap between theory and practice is subject. He also showed the agonized 'bourgeois conscience' to be more complex than the dismissive phraseology of 'intellectualism' or 'individualism' is capable of admitting.

The dilemmas of '*littérature engagée*' did not, of course, exist in isolation from the political situation itself. In practice, this meant that the 'agony' of responsibility and choice to which the existentialists felt themselves condemned, concerned their relations with the 'official' socialists, the Communists: was one with the *PCF* or against it? In effect, their answer was both yes and no. The aspiration to a 'third way' in politics was clearly expressed in the first issue of *Les Temps Modernes* – a magazine founded in 1945 by Sartre, Merleau-Ponty and others. Critical of all parties and committed to none, it tended none the less to support the USSR in the cold war. Hence the early departure from its editorial collective of Raymond Aron and Albert Ollivier, both of whom sided with the USA. Under the leadership of Merleau-Ponty, the political standpoint of the journal was defined throughout its early years by a critical sympathy for the policies of the *PCF*, even though very little of the actual practice of the *PCF* at the time corresponded to the 'completely experimental and voluntary' Marxism for which Merleau-Ponty argued.[5]

Relations between the editors of *Les Temps Modernes* and the *PCF* deteriorated rapidly with the rise of the existentialist movement, against whose 'decadent philosophy' the Communists mounted an increasingly virulent attack. Attempts by Sartre to clarify the existentialist position proved to no avail, and the Communist newspaper, *L'Humanité*, continued to regard the existentialists as lackeys either of Gaullism or of American imperialism.

In 1948 an attempt was made by Sartre and his colleagues to establish an independent political front in the form of the *Rassemblement Democratique Revolutionaire*. Pledging itself to the discovery of 'the great democratic tradition of revolutionary socialism', the *Rassemblement* called for a 'third way' between the 'rottenness of capitalist democracy . . . and the limitations of communism in its Stalinian form'.[6] It quickly became apparent, however, that financial and ideological interests were at work to push it definitively towards the right. Sartre became suspicious, refused to attend its much heralded 'International Day for Resistance to Dictatorship and War' (which did indeed turn out to be pro-American), and soon withdrew his support altogether. The failure of the *Rassemblement* brought to an end the attempts of the existentialists to create a new political movement. They had now, according to Sartre, become fellow-travellers of the *PCF* 'without anyone's having invited them on the trip'.[7] Shortly afterwards, however, the Korean War, apparently initiated by the USSR, was to present a major test of their allegiance. Merleau-Ponty counselled silence on the war in *Les Temps Modernes*, and shortly afterwards deserted the journal in favour of what Sartre called 'the inner life'.[8] One of the products of these years of relative withdrawal from politics was the development of the 'new liberalism' of Merleau-Ponty's *Adventures of the Dialectic*.

Throughout the 1940s, however, Merleau-Ponty defended a Marxist 'humanism' that was markedly anti-liberal. Thus we find him writing in *Humanism and Terror* that 'all discussion from a liberal perspective misses the problem since it professes to be relevant to a country which has made and intends to continue a revolution whereas liberalism excludes the revolutionary hypothesis'; and in an attempt to cleanse 'humanism' of the taint of bourgeois liberalism (and to dissociate it, too, from pacifism), he argues that the question is not whether communism respects the laws of liberalism, which it most evidently does not, but 'whether the violence it exercises is revolutionary and capable of creating human relations between men'.[9] So while Sartre was attempting to reassert the ethical basis of all revolutionary action ('the declaration that "we too are men" is at the bottom of any revolution', he wrote),[10] and was declaring the compatibility of Marxist class analysis with an all-embracing humanism, Merleau-Ponty was insisting upon the need to recognize violence against 'some men' as a condition of the realization of humanist principles. Anti-communists, he claimed, 'refuse to see that violence is universal' – one could not be of the party of progress without admitting the use of violence on behalf of 'progress'.[11]

In his essay on 'Bukharin and the Ambiguity of History' Merleau-Ponty tried to make sense of Bukharin's confession, at his trial, of charges that were patently fabricated. The trial, he argues, will only be comprehensible 'between revolutionaries . . . between men who are convinced they are making *history* and who consequently already see the present as past and see those who hesitate as traitors'.[12] Bukharin is therefore the victim of history's maleficence – which 'solicits men, tempts them so that they believe they are going in its direction, and then suddenly it unmasks and events change and prove there was another possibility'.[13] Bukharin's trial is for Merleau-Ponty a symbol of a 'counter-finality' in history – whereby in retrospect the intentions of our acts are stolen from us while at the same time we have, objectively, to acknowledge that 'they always meant' what they are eventually interpreted as meaning: 'the true nature of the tragedy appears once *the same man* has understood both that he cannot disavow the objective pattern of his actions, and that he is for others in the context of history, and yet that the motive of his actions constitutes a man's worth as he himself experiences it'.[14] Yet the 'objective pattern' that was Stalinism's contribution to 'reality' and to the 'tribunal of history' was, in the end, to be rejected by Merleau-Ponty himself precisely because it represented a betrayal of Marxism. The Marxist 'truth' had in the end proved 'false' because *it had not come out as intended*, and there could be no adjustment to the reality it had brought into being that could render it true.

The Korean War led to a vast disillusionment with the USSR among French intellectuals.[15] Sartre, however, did not move to the Right, and when it came to a final 'choosing of sides' opted for the *PCF* (the catalyst for his decision was the arrest in 1952 of its leader, Jacques Duclos). 'In the name of those principles which it had inculcated into me', he wrote, 'in the name of its humanism and its humanities, in the name of liberty, equality and fraternity, I swore to the bourgeoisie a hatred that would die only with me.'[16] After some prevarication, the *PCF* invited Sartre's participation, and from 1951–5, he wrote scarcely a word against either the party or the Soviet Union. Support for the USSR became marginally easier with death of Stalin in 1953 and the subsequent moderate programme of liberalization in the eastern bloc. All hopes of a definitive break with the past were to be shattered, however, by the Soviet invasion of Hungary in 1956. While remaining committed to Marxism, Sartre thereupon formally severed his relations with the *PCF*.

While the existentialists had attempted to develop a humanist critique of Marxism outside the *PCF*, others had been attempting a similar task from within. Naturally, their humanist campaign (which owed much to the championing by Lucien Goldmann – not himself a *PCF* member – of the doctrines of his Hungarian teacher, Lukács) was conducted in a rather muted and covert fashion.

As early as 1939, Henri Lefebvre had published a brief but revolutionary study of Marxist philosophy, *Le Materialisme Dialectique*. This argued, in a mild and abstract fashion, that the Marxist dialectic was based on concepts of alienation and *praxis* rather than on an Engelsian 'Dialectics of Nature', and drew extensively on the recently published *1844 Manuscripts* (which he was the first to translate into French).

It was not, however, until 1956, in the wake of the suppression of the Hungarian uprising, that the party dissidents developed a concerted and explicit attack upon orthodoxy. Their 'coming out' was marked by the foundation of the journal, *Arguments* (of which Lefebvre, Edgar Morin, Jean Duvigneaud, Kostas Axelos and Pierre Fougeyrollas – all of them members or former members of the *PCF* – were the initial editors), and this became a focus of a new Marxist–humanist critique of Stalinism.

Not surprisingly the *1844 Manuscripts* became a central reference point of the journal, and the influence of existentialism was extensive. Lefebvre looked to Sartre for a theory of alienation under capitalism which, he argued, encompassed the very styles of consumption, culture, systems of meaning and language of capitalist existence; others in the *Arguments* group were more influenced by Heidegger's attack on western metaphysics (an attack which, as we have seen, included Sartre himself within its compass). Kostas Axelos, for example, and Pierre Fougeyrollas both followed Heidegger in regarding Marxism as doomed by its traditional metaphysical outlook, and questioned the 'less than truly human' values of Marxist humanism.

Also influential upon the *Arguments* group, were the ex-Trotskyite theorists centred round the journal (founded by Cornelius Castoriadis and Claude Lefort), *Socialisme ou Barbarie*. Defined by unswerving opposition both to capitalism and to 'socialism' as practiced in the USSR (hence to the *PCF* and to the existentialists whom it regarded as compromised by their support for the Communists), *Socialisme ou Barbarie* had been pressing this double-edged attack since 1949. Starting from classical Marxist premises, they argued that Soviet socialism was a class society no less than western capitalism, and their relentless criticism of

Marxist practice eventually led them to reject the theory too. As one commentator has put it, 'For Castoriadis it was a matter of rejecting Marxism in order to remain revolutionary.'[17]

The Left as a whole repudiated the work of Castoriadis and Lefort, as lending itself to right-wing manipulation, and the *Socialisme ou Barbarie* group was neglected. After 1956, however, the apparent prescience of its attack on the USSR, and the correspondence of its theory of *autogestion* (workers' self-management) to the demands of the popular rebellions in eastern Europe increased its influence. The impact of its *gauchiste* critique of Marxism on the events of May 1968, and on subsequent criticisms of Marxist attitudes to power should not be underestimated.[18]

The politics of Marxist humanism

The decade following Stalin's death in 1953 saw a number of movements for liberalization in eastern Europe, all of them conducted in the name of 'humanism'. Though these movements were condemned in the 1950s by orthodox communism as 'revisionist', by the 1960s it was the Communists who were identifying themselves as 'humanists', and proclaiming a belief in 'Everything for Man'.

The two most important sources of this renaissance of Marxist humanism were, first, Khrushchev's denunciation of 'Stalinism' and the dissemination of two 'key' texts of humanist Marxism: *The Economic and Philosophical Manuscripts of 1844*, and the *Grundrisse*, a 1000-page collection of Marx's working notes for *Capital*.[19]

The publication in 1923 of Karl Korsch's *Marxism and Philosophy*, and Lukács's *History and Class Consciousness*, both of which emphasized Marx's debt to Hegel, had prepared the way, as we have noted, for a sympathetic reception of these works, and in eastern Europe after 1956 and *1844 Manuscripts* came to be used as a basis for opposition to Stalinism in a manner that has been compared to the use made of the New Testament in the Reformation.[20]

Not only in Hungary, but also in Poland, Yugoslavia and Czechoslovakia a new 'socialist humanist' movement was under way, in which demands 'from below' for workers' control were combining with the philosophical inspiration of the early Marxist texts to produce a vision of socialism that went far beyond Khrushchev's measured rejection of 'personality cults'. It was during this period that the Yugoslav philosophers, Mihailo Markovic and Gaia Petrovic first formulated the 'humanist' Marxism that was to draw within its orbit those who later formed the *Praxis* group;[21] that Leszek Kolakowski penned the attacks on 'Stalinism' that were to establish him as the philosophical spokesman of Polish 'revisionism';[22] and that the Czechoslovak, Karel Kosik, first launched the attack on communist 'dogmatism' that was elaborated in his important book of 1961, *Dialectics of the Concrete* (a sustained assertion of the importance of the individual and the 'human personality' in the making of history, that was subsequently to land him in jail).[23]

In Britain, there was little philosophical interest in the early works of Marx, and the debate over Marx's Hegelianism and humanism only really began to develop after 1960, and then mostly along lines already mapped out by continental Marxists. None the less, it was in the late 1950s that the English 'new left' came into being. This was based around two journals, *The New Reasoner* and *Universities and Left Review*, both of which expressed their commitment to 'socialist humanism' and which amalgamated in 1959 to form the *New Left Review* – an organ which described itself as a 'bi-monthly journal of Socialist Humanism'. The *Review* remained committed to that perspective until 1962, when its founding editors (led by E. P. Thompson, John Saville and Stuart Hall) were replaced by an editorial team headed by Perry Anderson.[24]

Throughout the 1950s, the official programme of de-Stalinization in eastern Europe and the Soviet Union went hand in hand with attacks on the works of the young Marx, and attempts were made to rescue an authentic, mature Marx from the 'Hegelianism' that his 'revisionist' humanist interpreters were imputing to him.

The maintenance of an ideological front that combined criticism of Stalin with the attack upon the anti-Stalinist 'humanist' revival proved difficult for the Soviet theoreticians. By 1960, in fact, it was decided that the Soviet Union had made the transition to a new stage of history. The 'class' humanism, based on dictatorship of the proletariat that it had been defending for forty years against bourgeois 'revisionist' humanism, was incompatible with the notion that the Soviet Union had transformed itself into a classless society. Under the slogan 'Everything for Man', a 'personal' humanism became the order of the day, based on respect for the freedom and worth of the individual 'as such'.

No sooner, however, had the Communists adjusted to the new circumstances than they found themselves attacked from the rear. For it was in the form of a condemnation of the 'phony communism', 'revisionism' and 'bourgeois humanism' of the Khrushchev regime's claims to have transcended class struggle, that the Chinese Communist Party offered its own redefinition of internationalism (according to which centuries rather than decades of class and ideological struggle were required for the establishment of socialism).

Launched in 1960 on the occasion of Lenin's birthday with the famous *Red Flag* editorial 'Long Live Leninism!', the Chinese attack on Soviet humanism was pursued with increasing vigour over the next four years, and indeed broadened into a denial of the whole idea of 'Marxist humanism'. In the words of a speech by Chou Yang in 1963 to the Department of Philosophy and Social Sciences in the Chinese Academy of Science:

The modern revisionists and some bourgeois scholars try to describe Marxism as humanism and call Marx a humanist. Some people counterpose the young Marx to the mature proletarian revolutionary Marx. In particular they make use of certain views on 'alienation' expressed by Marx in his early *Economic and Philosophic Manuscripts, 1844* to depict him as an exponent of the bourgeois theory of human nature. They do their best to preach so-called Humanism by using the concept of alienation. This, of course, is futile.[25]

As a 'philosophical' dispute, the Sino-Soviet conflict was somewhat lacking in sophistication. To attempt, for example, to define the Marxist dialectic as a 'unity of opposites' was supposedly to reveal one's sympathies for Russia.[26] The motives for the dispute were, in fact, quite nakedly political. The Chinese were hoping to promote the idea of a third force, based on a Chinese-Indonesian alliance, to which the countries of the Third World and all those genuinely opposed to American imperialism would turn for leadership; and their denial of the relevance of the concepts of alienation and humanism was timely given the severity of the demands to which the Chinese people were expected voluntarily to submit for the sake of the required leap in productivity.

Blind as it may have been, the commitment to Maoism in certain sections of the European Left was understandable. To those who felt that the revolutionary principles of Marxism had as little to do with the woolly and abstract 'humanism' in the name of which Khrushchev was actively seeking peaceful coexistence with the capitalists and imperialists, as it had to do with Stalin's purges, it had obvious appeal; while for those who had come to disparage as purely academic the question of what constituted a 'genuine' Marxist practice, but who were none the less disaffected with the values of their own capitalist society, China was far enough away and different enough to serve as the Utopia by reference to which one could vent one's spleen on every manifestation of western decadence (socialist organizations included).[27] Furthermore, the Maoist Cultural Revolution of 1966-9 placed a gratifying emphasis on political and cultural activity.

This was the context, then, in which Louis Althusser intervened on behalf of 'Marxist anti-humanism' in 1961-2.[28] Though he had been a member of the *PCF* since 1948, he disagreed with the pro-Russian stance of the party, which was now, of course, preaching the gospel of 'Marxist humanism', and thus lending itself to the distortion of Marxism by those who were finding in the *1844 Manuscripts* and other works confirmation and endorsement of those very bourgeois pieties that Marx wrote *Capital* in order to dispel. Most alarming to Althusser in this respect was the growing Catholic interest in Marx as represented by Calvez, Bigo, Rubel, Cornu[29] and within the party most notably by Garaudy[30] – at whose hands, so it has been said, Marx began to look like 'a gentle idealist, or a sentimental anarchist or fastidious aesthete, rather than the prototype of a stern, disciplined and dutiful member of a centralised Marxist-Leninist party'.[31] Althusser's anti-humanism, therefore, began life as a multifaceted ideological-political intervention, aimed at rescuing Marxism from its deviations into Stalinism (economism), on the one hand, and into social democratic reformism (Hegelian-humanism), on the other.[32]

The events of May 1968 were seen by many (though not by those in the *PCF*) as a concrete expression of the themes of humanist Marxism – as an assertion of the powers of the human subject against the 'alienations' of capitalist society. For while the anti-humanist 'structuralists' had been systematically rejecting the category of 'the subject' in theory, those 'subjects' were spontaneously taking to the streets, and adopting slogans directly associating structuralism with bourgeois and bureaucratic authoritarianism. 'Revolution must be made in men, before it can be made in things', they proclaimed, parrying Foucault's neo-Nietzschean affirmation of the 'Death of Man' (though hardly transcending its sexism);[33] against the 'dictatorship of the signifier' they advocated the *prise de parôle*; against structuralist aridity and theoreticism, they asserted the fertility of the imagination.

But the spirit of May 1968 was not to be sustained. And it was its anarchism (which led to the refusal of many of the participants in the May events to sully themselves with the party politics that might have removed the Gaullists from power) which proved its undoing. At the philosophical level, therefore, while the May events might be taken as exemplifying the Sartrean 'fused-group', thereby vindicating the humanist theory of revolution as the transcendence by massed individuals of their 'serial' grouping, it was equally a demonstration of the limits of existentialist Marxism. For while Sartre had argued that the source of the corruption and distortion of the revolutionary 'moment' lay in the institutionalization of politics (the tendency of 'fused groups' to collapse into seriality), it was the very fear of bureaucratization that prevented the activists in the May events from consolidating their power in any institutional form, and thus led to the dissolution of the 'revolution' itself. It must be said, however, that in the eyes of the *PCF* and the majority of workers, the situation was never even potentially 'revolutionary'.

In the wake of the May events, the 'structuralists' began to receive a more respectful hearing, and themselves made a number of concessions to the humanists. The leading lights of anti-humanism (with the exception of Lévi-Strauss) had never themselves been very happy with the 'structuralist' label. In the *Archaeology of Knowledge* (which appeared in France in 1969), Foucault goes to some pains to dissociate himself from the structuralist movement; Althusser, likewise professed himself at most a 'pseudo-structuralist' and after 1968 engaged in a number of self-criticisms and corrections of misinterpretations on this score. His pupil, Nico Poulantzas, whose anti-subjectivist interpretation and elaboration of the Marxist theory of the State has had a strong influence on the theory and practice of Eurocommunism, went even further in his rejection of his early structuralist leanings. Prior to his suicide in 1979, Poulantzas was polemicizing directly with Foucault, and just before his death wrote that

In the theoretical conjuncture in which we were working it was structuralism against historicism, it was Lévi-Strauss against Sartre. It has been extremely difficult for us to make a total rupture from these two problematics. We insisted that for Marxism the main danger was not structuralism but historicism itself. So we directed all our attention against historicism – the problematic of the subject; against the problematics of Sartre and Lukács, and as a result we 'bent the stick'; and of course this had had effects in our theory itself.[34]

The extent to which Althusser himself has reneged on previously held positions must remain unclear.[35] Some have argued[36] that by the late 1970s he had been forced to beat a retreat to the phenomenological Marxism he had spent his intellectual life attacking. For the record, we should add that belatedly (far too belatedly some would argue)[37] Althusser did cast off the veils of theoreticism that for so long mediated such criticism as he was prepared to make of the *PCF*, and made a frank attack on it in April 1978.

The developments surveyed in this chapter suggest that 1968 was something of a watershed for both the political practice and the philosophical concerns of the intellectual Left in France in the post-war period. For many Marxists, it meant a break with Soviet communism, and a move towards the Eurocommunism which was to be developed by western European communist parties in the 1970s. The other political legacy of 1968 has been the creation of various pressure-groups and parties working for many of the demands that existed only as a cultural and somewhat ephemeral 'humanist' protest in 1968. The consolidation of the feminist movement and the formation of a 'green' political front are the most striking examples.

At the philosophical level, the 'self-criticism' of the structuralists set the stage for the emergence of a 'post-structuralism' which remains as hostile as ever to the 'humanist' problematic of the subject, but which combines this with an attack upon the ahistoric rationalism, scientism, of the structuralists themselves (who are held to be damned, therefore, along with the humanists, by virtue of their implicit acceptance of the framework of western metaphysics). The quest for identity, whether of structures or of subjects, is replaced by the assertion of difference. In the name of difference, an attack has been mounted on synthesis and generalization as such. For the post-structuralists, the ideal of 'reason' must itself be overhauled as a condition of . . . one cannot say of what, since their attack casts doubt on every possible goal including truth itself. Post-structuralism is discussed further in Chapter 6.

Notes

1 See K. Kautsky, *The Economic Doctrines of Karl Marx* (London 1925); N. Bukharin, *Historical Materialism* (New York 1925); Plekhanov,

Fundamental Problems of Marxism (London 1937); J. Stalin, 'Dialectical and Historical Materialism', ch. IV of *History of the CPSU (B)* (Moscow 1940).
2 Unpublished notes cited in Simone de Beauvoir, *The Prime of Life*, trans. Peter Green (London 1962).
3 By Ronald Aronson in his account (see ch. 8) of Sartre's life and work, *Jean-Paul Sartre, Philosophy in the World* (London 1980), p. 8. I have drawn extensively in this chapter on this work, and on M.-A. Burnier, *Choice of Action*, trans. Bernard Murchland (New York 1968).
4 See Sartre's articles for *Les Lettres françaises*, 1943-5.
5 Maurice Merleau-Ponty, *'Pour la verité'*, *Les Temps Modernes*, no. 4 (January 1946).
6 J.-P. Sartre, G. Rosenthal, D. Rousset, *Entretiens sur la politique* (Paris 1949), p. 135. On the history and fate of the *RDR*, see Burnier, *Choice of Action*, pp. 54-6 and Aronson, *Jean-Paul Sartre*, pp. 163-5.
7 'Merleau-Ponty' in *Situations*, III, p. 259; de Beauvoir, *Force of Circumstance*, trans. R. Howard (London 1965), p. 176.
8 'Merleau-Ponty', *Situations*, p. 273.
9 M. Merleau-Ponty, *Humanism and Terror*, trans. J. O'Neill (Evanston 1964), pp. xvii-xviii. This work is comprised of a series of essays first written for *Les Temps Modernes* 1946-7 under the title *'Le Yogi et le Prolétaire'*.
10 Sartre, *Literary and Philosophical Essays*, p. 217.
11 Merleau-Ponty, *Humanism and Terror*, p. 2.
12 ibid., p. 29; see also Sonia Kruks, *The Political Philosophy of Merleau-Ponty* (Brighton 1981), pp. 39-40; 89-91.
13 Merleau-Ponty, *Humanism and Terror*, p. 29.
14 ibid., p. 62.
15 In 'Merleau-Ponty', *Situations*, p. 198, Sartre speaks of the 'instant' of Korea as revealing to Merleau-Ponty the full horror of Stalinism. For discussion of Merleau-Ponty's rejection of Marxism, see Kruks, *Political Philosophy*, chs 6 and 7. See also Burnier, *Choice of Action*, part II, ch. 1.
16 'Merleau-Ponty' *Situations*, pp. 287-8.
17 A. Hirsh, *The French New Left* (London 1982), p. 112 (and see also pp. 146-7; 197-200). Castoriadis's attack on Marxism was developed in a series of articles written 1964-5 which now form the first part of *L'Institution imaginaire de la société*. The critique is pursued

further in *Les carrefours du labyrinthe* (Paris 1978) (*The Crossroads in the Labyrinth*, trans. by Kate Soper and Martin H. Ryle (Brighton 1983)).

18 Both Bernard-Henri Lévy (see *Barbarism with a Human Face* (New York 1979)) and André Glucksmann (see *The Master Thinkers* (New York 1980)), leading lights of the 'New Philosophy', have been influenced by the *Socialisme ou Barbarie* analysis, even though their disillusionment with Marxism owes most to Nietzsche and Foucault.

19 It was not until 1927 that a complete edition of the early writings, including the *Economic and Philosophic Manuscripts*, was published by the Marx–Engels Institute in Moscow, edited by D. Ryazanov. This edition (though not its influence) was discontinued for political reasons after 1932. In the 1950s it was, for the most part, only the Frankfurt school of Marxists who paid any serious attention to the *Grundrisse*. A full text in English was not published until 1973 (trans. Martin Nicolaus (Penguin and New Left Books)). For a brief discussion of the reception of the early Marxist texts, see David McLellan, *Marx before Marxism* (Harmondsworth 1970), ch. 8; also Perry Anderson, *Considerations on Western Marxism* (London 1974), pp. 50–5.

20 McLellan, *Marx before Marxism*, p. 274.

21 For accounts of the Praxis school of humanist Marxism in Yugoslavia, see *Praxis*, ed. Mihailo Markovic and Gaia Petrovic (Reidel 1979); and *Marxist Humanism and Praxis*, ed. G. Sher (Buffalo 1978). Their work is also sympathetically discussed in Raya Dunayevskaya, *Philosophy and Revolution* (New York 1973), pp. 252–4, and represented in Erich Fromm, *Socialist Humanism* (Harmondsworth 1967). Their journal, *Praxis*, is now published in Serbo-Croat and English, and distributes internationally. For news and reviews relating to the Praxis group, see *Radical Philosophy* nos. 28 and 30.

22 A teacher of philosophy at Warsaw University until he left Poland in 1968, Leszek Kolakowski gave passionate and eloquent expression to the feelings that led to the Polish 'October' of 1956 in two essays ('What is Socialism?' and 'The End of the Age of Myths') which remained unpublished in Poland. His remarkable polemic, 'Responsibility and History' (first published in *Nowa Kultura* (1957)) is included along with other writings dating to the late 1950s in *Marxism and Beyond*, trans. Jane Zielonko Peel and intro. Leopold

Labedz (London 1969). Though in these essays he deplores the 'transformation of dissidents into renegades', and speaks of socialist criticism as 'indispensable for an effective opposition to real counter-revolutionary criticism' (p. 126), since moving to the West (he is now a Fellow of All Souls, Oxford), Kolakowski has ceased to defend a socialist position. E. P. Thompson remonstrates with him in his 'Open Letter to Kolakowski', *The Poverty of Theory* (London 1978), pp. 93-192.

23 The influence of Karel Kosik's *Dialectics of the Concrete* (1961) (Reidel 1976), is discussed in Dunayevskaya's chapter on 'State Capitalism and the East European Revolts', in *Philosophy and Revolution*.

24 *The New Reasoner* (originally entitled the *Reasoner*) was established as a journal for Communist dissidents in the wake of suppression of the Hungarian uprisings in 1956 (when some 10,000, or a third of the membership, left the British Communist Party). The *Universities and Left Review* began life in 1957 under the editorship of Stuart Hall, Gabriel Pearson, Ralph Samuel and Charles Taylor. For a sense of the differences which split the 'new Left' and established the *New Left Review* (*NLR*) under Anderson's editorship, see E. P. Thompson, 'The peculiarities of the English', *The Poverty of Theory*, pp. 35-91; Perry Anderson, 'Origins of the Present Crisis', *NLR*, no. 23 (January-February 1964); Tom Nairn, 'The English Working Class', *NLR*, no. 24 (March-April 1964). See also Jonathan Rée, 'Socialist Humanism', *Radical Philosophy*, no. 7 (winter 1974), pp. 33-6.

25 Cited in Dunayevskaya, pp. 181-2.

26 ibid., pp. 182-4; see also Jonathan Rée, 'Philosophy in China - what can we learn from it?' in *Radical Philosophy*, no. 14 (summer 1976), p. 20f.

27 Jonathan Rée, 'Philosophy in China', draws attention to the parallel between the 'Chinese utopias' projected by the Enlightenment thinkers in the eighteenth century and the similar function they served as outlets for resentment and denunciation of everything close to home.

28 Althusser's articles of 1961-3 were first published together in *Pour Marx* (1966). In a preface written for the English translation (*For Marx* (London 1969)), Althusser reminds his English readers that 'to understand these essays and to pass judgement on them, it is essential to realise that they were conceived, written and published

by a Communist philosopher in a particular ideological and theoretical conjuncture' and goes on to relate his intervention to the ideological effects of a certain complicity in the use of the slogans of 'humanism' for political ends by both the CPSU and by western communist parties in their quest for 'unity with socialists, democrats and Catholics' and a 'peaceful transition to socialism' (see pp. 10–11).

29 See J. Y. Calvez, *La Pensée de Karl Marx* (Paris 1956); M. Rubel, Introduction to Karl Marx, *Oeuvres*, vol. 2 (Paris 1946); A. Cornu, *Karl Marx et Friedrich Engels, Leur vie et oeuvre*, 4 vols. (Paris 1955–70).

30 Roger Garaudy, *De l'anathème au dialogue* (Paris 1965), and *Marxisme de XXe siècle* (Paris 1966). In both these works, communism and catholicism are presented as sharing a common humanist framework of aspirations.

31 Jonathan Rée, 'The Anti-Althusser Bandwagon', *Radical Science Journal*, (1981), no. 11.

32 Althusser was attacked by Garaudy and other party intellectuals, who were fearful of his influence within the party's student organization. Readjustment followed fairly swiftly, however, partly because Althusser was ready to pay for his delinquency with some professions of self-criticism and to remain within the *PCF* despite its expulsion of 600 of its Maoist sympathizers; partly because the *PCF* itself came to realize that the credibility of its somewhat threadbare defence of orthodoxy could be served rather than damaged by investment in some Althusserian refinements. See Hirsh, *The French New Left*, pp. 167–71.

33 No doubt to the disgust of some of the female participants in the de-reification of politics, and who were later, in the light of the male dominated humanism of May 1968 to work, albeit very critically at times, on the bases established by Simone de Beauvoir in the 1950s, to establish an organized feminist movement in France.

34 Stuart Hall and Alan Hunt, 'Interview with Nicos Poulantzas', *Marxism Today* (July 1979), p. 198.

35 In 1980 Althusser killed his wife and was committed to a mental asylum.

36 The most eloquent and relentless attack to date on Althusser's prolonged silence (indeed upon the entire Althusserian edifice) is by E. P. Thompson, *The Poverty of Theory*, pp. 193–406. For some discussion of this polemic, and the motives for it, see Chapter 5.

37 For a fuller account, see Paul Patton, *Radical Philosophy* 'News', no. 21 (spring 1979), and Hirsh, *The French New Left*, pp. 201–4; see also

The Poverty of Theory (postscript), and Perry Anderson, *Arguments within English Marxism* (London 1980), pp. 112-16.

Further reading

For further information on Sartre's career and its intellectual and political context, see Simone de Beauvoir's memoirs: *The Prime of Life*, trans. Peter Green (London 1962); *Force of Circumstance*, trans. Richard Howard (London 1965), and *Adieux: a farewell to Sartre*, trans. Patrick O'Brian (London 1984) (recollections and conversations with Sartre dating to the 1970s). See also Sartre's plays and novels and his own autobiographical work, *Words* (1964), trans. Irene Clephane (London 1964).

On the politics of post-war existentialism in France see the works cited in the bibliography to Chapter 2 and in note 3 of this chapter. David Caute addresses the subject in *Existential Marxism in France: from Sartre to Althusser* (Princeton 1975), and Rosanna Rosandra has an interesting article on 'Sartre's political practice' in *The Socialist Register* (1975). A general overview of Left-wing thought and activity in France from the end of the war until 1968 is provided by Arthur Hirsh, *The French New Left* (London 1982). For a participant's reflections and analysis of the events of 1968, see André Glucksmann, 'Strategy and Revolution in France', *New Left Review*, no. 52 (November–December, 1968) (this is a special issue devoted to May 1968).

Works by members of the *Arguments* group include: Henri Lefebvre, *The Sociology of Marx*, trans. N. Guterman (London 1968), *Everyday Life in the Modern World* (London 1971), *The Survival of Capitalism*, trans. Frank Bryant (London 1976); Kostas Axelos, *Marx, penseur de la technique* (Paris 1961); Pierre Fougeyrollas, *Le Marxisme en question* (Paris 1960). A brief discussion of the *Socialisme ou barbarie* group is included in Hirsh, *The French New Left*, pp. 108–31.

Further illustration of the 'humanist' Marxism developed in eastern Europe after Stalin's death is to be found in the essays in *The Humanisation of Socialism*, ed. A. Hegedus (London 1978); in Gaia Petrovic, *Marx in the mid-Twentieth Century* (London 1967); and in Mihailo Markovic, *The Contemporary Marx, Essays on Humanist Communism* (London 1974).

5
The death of 'Marxist Man'

It would be a mistake to identify 'anti-humanism' with Louis Althusser's reading of Marx. For Althusser was only applying to Marxism ideas which were generated outside it, and whose main line of development runs from the structuralist anthropology of Claude Lévi-Strauss, through the work of Jacques Lacan and Michel Foucault, to the radical anti-subjectivism of Derridean 'post-structuralism'.

Structuralism and post-structuralism comprise a number of heterogeneous theories linked by a commitment to semiology and to the mode of study of human culture which it introduces. According to the semiologist, the traditional human sciences have failed in their task, because they have overlooked the dimension of representation from within which they have 'observed' their subject matter. The visual metaphor is, however, misleading, since the level of signification to which semiology directs attention is not to be compared to a lens through which we 'see' to that beyond and outside it and whose specific distortions we are therefore able in principle to acknowledge and take account of. Even 'representation' is a misnomer if it is taken to imply the imaging or depicting of something other than itself, of which it is the mere vehicle for expression; for what the semiological perspective invites us to understand is that meanings are constitutive of human reality itself, not its mediation. There is no ulterior reality prior to and standing 'behind' the signs which denote it.

In pointing this out, semiology is not committed to the position sometimes attributed to it, of an idealist denial of the 'outside world', but only to what might seem a more Kantian insistence upon the symbolically constituted nature of all human experience. The very structures of human culture, Lacan has claimed, 'reveal an ordering of possible exchanges which, even if unconscious, is inconceivable outside the permutations authorised by language', and he goes on to suggest that a comprehension based on the two-dimensional flatness of 'nature versus culture' must be supplanted by a three-dimensional model of understanding:

the ethnographic duality of nature and culture is giving way to a ternary conception of the human condition – nature, society and culture – the last term of which could well be reduced to language, or that which essentially distinguished human society from natural societies.[1]

Foucault argues for similar ternary conception. He insists that it is neither biology, nor economics nor even philology that comprise the objects of the human sciences, but our representations to ourselves of the activities they study.[2] The proper concern of these sciences, he says, is not with the function of sexuality, but with the way it is lived; not with the function of the exchange of goods, but with the way in which individuals or groups represent to themselves the partners with whom they produce or exchange; not with language, but with the way in which human beings represent words to themselves, utilize their forms and meanings to compose discourse.

The human sciences, then, are not an analysis of what humanity is 'by nature', but of what enables 'man in his positivity (living, speaking, labouring, being) to know (or seek to know) what life is, in what the essence of labour and its laws consist, and in what way he is able to speak'. In Foucault's definition, man is 'that living being who, from within the life to which he entirely belongs and by which he is traversed in his whole being, constitutes representations by means of which he lives, and on the basis of which he possesses that strange capacity of being able to represent to himself this life itself'.[3]

It is thus our existence as sign users – or, in Barthes's tag, *'homo significans'* – that becomes the focus of interest. Whether the particular engagement is with the linguistic sign itself (Saussure, Derrida); or with myth (Lévi-Strauss); or with the unconscious (Lacan); or with human communication in literature, dress and gesture – the word and sign created worlds to which Barthes has drawn attention; or (as with Foucault), the mutations in the forms of representation itself, and the specific discourses to which they give rise – in all these cases, the concern is with the universal inscription of humankind within language and systems of codification which regulate all human experience and activity, and therefore lie beyond the control of either individuals or social groups.

Anti-historicism: Lévi-Strauss's attack on Sartre

If, as we have suggested, the mainstream of structuralist and post-structuralist thinking has had little to do with Marxism, we should not forget that when Lévi-Strauss launched the 'slogan of the decade'[4] with his pronouncement that the goal of the human sciences was 'not to constitute but to dissolve man', it was in the context of a direct attack upon Sartre's theorization of the Marxian dialectic in the *Critique of Dialectical Reason*.[5] Nor should we underestimate the influence of this attack upon the development of Althusser's own brand of Marxism.

The importance of Lévi-Strauss's challenge to Sartre's 'historicism' lay in the manner in which it brought into focus the fundamental connection between the claim that 'men make history' and the argument that history itself is possessed of its own irreducible 'dialectic' or intelligibility. For the humanist, the meaning, continuity and purpose attributed to collective human action are intrinsic components of 'history', comprehensible only to *historical* understanding. Naturalistic attempts to explain such action are therefore profoundly mistaken: 'history' is neither reducible to biology (and thus ultimately to psychology and physiology) nor reabsorbable within a more general evolutionary theory or cosmology.[6] What humanist thought therefore wishes to preserve – and to demarcate in the distinction between 'made' and 'unmade' eventuation – is a difference of kind between 'history' and 'pre-history', between the 'human' and the 'natural'.

In rejecting this humanist argument, Lévi-Strauss argued that to privilege history in this fashion was to cast it in the role of myth. The humanists, according to him, were simply repeating the error of Descartes's *cogito* on a macrocosmic scale: they were treating the experience of history as if it provided access to a self-validating truth. In reality, the human sciences could only claim to be 'scientific' if they undertook to penetrate beneath this illusion of historical understanding and to reveal the ahistoric unconscious which underlies its ethnocentric representations. Only thus might they arrive at the truth which historical reason systematically represses – the truth, namely, that there is no difference between logical and prelogical thought, and therefore no final demarcation to be drawn between the 'civilized' and the 'primitive', the 'developed' and the 'undeveloped'. For we must understand that history is 'tied neither to man nor to any particular object', but consists entirely in its method:

We need only recognise that history is a method with no distinct object corresponding to it to reject the equivalence between the notion of history and the notion of humanity which some have tried to foist on us with the unavowed aim of making historicity the last refuge of a transcendental humanism: as if men could regain the illusion of liberty on the plane of the 'we' merely by giving up the 'I's that are too obviously wanting in consistency.[7]

History, in short, does not record or discover meaning; it does no more than provide a catalogue which can serve as a point of departure in the quest for intelligibility. We must understand, that is, that there has been no progress of the kind that humanist historians suppose, no development of cognition, no dialectical process at work in human society, but merely the reformulation in numerous different guises of an essential structure of human knowledge – a structure which is, according to Lévi-Strauss, a closed system. Historical thought is simply the humanist mythology by means of which the 'civilized' or 'developed' world relates to the discontinuous, objective and immutable structure of brain and psyche.

The 'errors' of Marx's humanist 'partisans'

Althusser's repeated denunciations of 'history' and his attacks upon Sartrean Marxism clearly testify to the influence of Lévi-Strauss's structuralism upon his own orientation. But in placing Althusserian Marxism in this context, we should distinguish between the argument of the essays in *For Marx* and the anti-humanist theory elaborated subsequently in *Reading Capital* and in *Lenin and Philosophy and Other Essays*.[8] More directly concerned in the later works with the theory of the 'subject', Althusser is also more explicit in revealing the links between his own warrant for the death of Man and those issued by non-Marxist structuralists. *For Marx*, on the other hand, concentrates upon the error of those who regard the 'humanism' of Marx's early texts as providing the key to his mature theory. Althusser's most immediate concern in this work is to convince us that Marx's later argument is not only fundamentally discontinuous with his earlier theory, but is in every way superior to it.

How far the older Marx is to be charged with the deeds of the younger is to be settled, according to Althusser, by consideration of the role played by the concept of alienation. As an ethical concept, this can play no part, he insists, in scientific understanding. So to claim that Marx's conception of history depends upon it, is to deny that historical materialism can be scientific. The argument is summed up in the entry under 'alienation' in the glossary to the English translations of Althusser's work:

ALIENATION: an ideological concept used by Marx in his Early Works and regarded by the partisans of those works as the key concept of Marxism. Marx derived the term from Feuerbach's anthropology where it denoted the state of man and society where the essence of man is only present to him in the distorted form of a god, which, although man created it in the image of his essence (his species-being), appears to him as an external, pre-existing creator. Marx used the concept to criticize the State and the economy as confiscating the real self-determining labour of men in the same way. In his later works, however, the term appears very rarely, and where it does it is either used ironically, or with a different conceptual content (in *Capital*, for instance).

As for the 'partisans' of these Early Works, Althusser writes:

The position is quite clearly put: *Capital* is an ethical theory, the silent philosophy of which is openly spoken in Marx's Early Works. This, reduced to two propositions, is the thesis which has had such extraordinary success. And not only in France and Italy, but also . . . in contemporary Germany and Poland. Philosophers, ideologues, theologians have all launched into a gigantic enterprise of criticism and conversion: let Marx be restored to his source, and let him admit at last that in him, the mature man is merely the young man in disguise. Or if he stubbornly insists on his age, let him admit the sins of his maturity, let him recognise that he sacrified philosophy to economics, ethics to science and man to history. Whether he consent to it or refuse it, his truth, and everything that will survive him, everything which helps the men that are to live and think, is contained in these few Early Works (*FM*, p. 52).

By imposing an Hegelian framework on Marx's theoretical development, the humanists not only fail to detect the 'break' between Feuerbachian and Marxist materialism, they also give Marxist theory a Hegelian content. Those who assert alienation to be the guiding thread through the Marxist corpus, have done no more, Althusser claims, than substitute the 'Human Essence' for the 'Absolute Idea'. History still has a subject – Man – whose drama unfolds within it: it is the predetermined progress through alienation to the realization of human species-being.

According to Althusser, however, Marx broke decisively with Hegelianism in 1845. Althusser tells us that this 'break' is marked by three indissociable elements: *a* the formation of a theory of history and politics based on radically new concepts (those of 'mode of production', 'forces of production', 'relations of production'); *b* a radical critique of the *theoretical* pretensions of philosophical humanism; *c* the definition of humanism as ideology. Together they amount to Marx's scientific discovery – a discovery that severs Marxism not only from the 'pre-Marxist' writings of Marx himself, but from all preceding bourgeois philosophy. For bourgeois philosophy, we learn, despite its various guises, conforms throughout to a 'humanist type structure'; it subscribes, that is, to two fundamental 'postulates': that there is 'a universal essence of man' and that this essence is 'the attribute of each single individual'. All the principal theories of society (Hobbes to Rousseau), of political economy (Petty to Ricardo) and of ethics (Descartes to Feuerbach via Kant) are founded in consequence on a false 'empiricist–idealist world outlook'. For

> If the essence of man is to be a universal attribute, it is essential that *concrete subjects* exist as absolute givens; this implies an *empiricism of the subject*. If these empirical individuals are to be men, it is essential that each carries in himself the whole human essence, if not in fact, at least in principle; this implies an *idealism of the essence*. So empiricism of the subject implies idealism of the essence and vice-versa. This relation can be inverted into its 'opposite' – empiricism of the concept/idealism of the subject. But the inversion respects the basic structure of the problematic, which remains fixed. (*FM*, p. 228)

What Althusser appears to be objecting to here is a 'humanist' conflation of the 'concrete (human) individual' with that of the 'human subject': where the humanists go wrong is in assimilating human biological entities (which are 'given') to 'subjects of experience' (which Althusser says are far from 'given', but on the contrary 'socially constituted'). His argument is that concrete individuals only become human 'subjects' in society, and that everything designated by the concept of 'subjectivity' (consciousness, experience, belief, attitude, the sense of self as a unity) is therefore a social effect. This means, in fact, that human subjects must be viewed as 'ideologically' constructed, 'ideology' being the term by which Althusser designates the representation of our relations to the conditions of our existence in the form of subjectivity: it is in 'ideology', says Althusser, that we become subjects, and since we cannot but think of ourselves as subjects, we cannot but live in ideology.[9]

In dismissing the humanist 'type structure', Althusser is therefore rejecting the idea that we can base social knowledge in our experience of ourselves as subjects. Since experience is, by definition, what subjects have, and subjects are ideological constructs, it is impossible for subjects as such to have genuine knowledge. Any theory (Hobbes, Descartes, Rousseau, Kant . . .) which invokes the category of the subject as if it were epistemologically fundamental (as if subjects *could* arrive at knowledge) is itself ideological, since it takes the subject to be the source of that which is reflected in its 'knowledge'.

Althusser also claims that the humanist type structure cannot theorize the conditions of existence of subjects: it has to take their existence as given. But subjects could be given in this way only on the basis of an *a priori* conception of what it is to be human – on the basis of an ideal of the 'truly human'. In rejecting humanist theory as 'ideological' Althusser is therefore also attacking it for concealment of its purely ethical status: while claiming to provide knowledge, philosophical anthropology of the kind embodied in the theory of alienation does no more than valorize existing or future conditions of existence, projecting them as an ideal essence of the human.

This argument, of course, makes use of the highly debatable assumption that ethical and scientific discourse are mutually exclusive. But even if we accept that the theory of alienation is an ethical theory which Marx himself later rejected, it by no means follows that ethical argument is absent from Marx's mature works. This might seem an obvious enough point to make given the abundance of normative themes in *Capital* and the relative dearth of references to alienation, but it has often been overlooked. In part the 'humanists' are themselves to blame for this conflation of issues, since they have tended to respond to Althusser *not* on the grounds that he falsely assumes that social theory can and should dispense with ethical discourse, but on the grounds that the theory of alienation is itself explanatory in a scientific sense. But if it is explanatory, it is so only in the sense that it conceptualizes the subordination of the 'authors and actors' of history to the processes of their own making. Moreover, in so far as the theory implies that a non-alienated society is one in which we shall have escaped all 'de-humanizing' forms of social mediation (private property, exchange relations, the money system), and will be able to relate to each other as the social individuals we are 'by nature' (i.e. simply 'as people')[10] it does conflict with the argument of historical materialism that individuals never relate simply as 'natural' beings. Slave and master, serf and feudal lord, capitalist and worker, the members of a socialist co-operative – all equally relate to each other 'as people' in the sense that they treat each other as human rather than as animal or inanimate entities, and no distinction can be drawn at this level of relations between what is 'human' and what is 'de-humanizing'.

To be told that 'man himself should be the intermediary between men' or that 'men should relate to each other as men'[11] is not, in fact, to be told anything specific about the form their interaction should take. This is the paradox about the theory of alienation. In positing an ideal of society in which social relations become interpersonal relations, in which 'de-institutionalized' individuals simply live 'as individuals' it upholds a vision of harmonious, non-exploitative relations but has nothing to tell us about the form which social relations must take in order for it to be realized. As one commentator has put it:

> The phrases 'man himself' and 'as people' trade on some *untheorised* ideal of the *really human*, some vision of *true humanity* being expressed in social life. They are functioning as metaphors in which idealised relations between *individuals* are illicitly mapped onto a utopian scheme of patterns of relations in general, relations in which social organisations (political organisations, institutions, collectivities of all kinds) have entirely disappeared. The disjunction between 'the human' and 'the de-humanized' as forms of social mediation, is empty of cognitive content, for the valorization of the former is based on nothing more than an implicit, essentialist individualist philosophical imperative.[12]

None of this, however, need force us to accept Althusser's interpretation of historical materialism as 'value-free science' nor his suggestion that *Capital* is free of moral argument. What it suggests, rather, is the necessity of establishing the relations between evaluative and non-evaluative discourse within Marxism. We can acknowledge the problems posed by Marx's account of 'non-alienated' society, while at the same time insisting that the normative discourse of *Capital* is very largely concerned with revealing the ways in which capitalist production is experienced as a natural process 'taking place behind the backs' of those who sustain it, but whose concerted actions alone make it possible.

Capitalist society, according to Marx, does indeed have a 'mastery over man' – it does not merely *seem* to have it – but it is a 'mastery' dependent on the experience of those it 'masters'. Marx presents the power of capitalist society as reliant on systematic misrepresentation of the role of human agency in the processes that maintain it. At the same time, the normative argument of *Capital* presumes that it is both desirable and possible that human beings should control the forces which determine their lives, and that knowledge is essential to the exercise of that control.

According to the Althusserian account, however, this appeal to human cognition and action is fundamentally misconceived. For it relies on the mistaken idea that human beings are the ultimate 'subjects' of the social processes in which they are enmeshed.

Althusserianism and the theory of the 'subject'

Althusser's account of the subject can be summed up in two theses: the first claims that individuals are not constitutive of the social process, but its 'supports' or 'effects'; the second that the subjectivity of the subject is constructed in ideology.

The argument for the first thesis is put in *Reading Capital* as follows:

> . . . the structure of the relations of production determines the *places* and *functions* occupied and adopted by the agents of production, who are never anything more than the occupants of these places, insofar as they are the supports (*Träger*) of these functions. The true 'subjects' (in the sense of the constitutive subjects of the process) are therefore not these occupants or functionaries, are not, despite all appearances, the 'real men' – but the *definition and its distribution of these places and functions. The true 'subjects' are these definers and distributors: the relations of production* (and political and ideological social relations.) But since these are 'relations', they cannot be thought within the category *subject*. (*RC*, p. 180)

Althusser here appears to deny the efficacy of human subjects upon history, treating them as 'supports' for relations created quite independently of their actions. But this view has no support in Marx's own writing. It is true that Marx used the word '*Träger*' on occasion.

It is also true that he claims that in *Capital* he treats individuals 'only insofar as they are personifications of economic categories, embodiments of particular class-relations and class-interests'.[13] But this does not imply that individuals are *nothing but* 'personifications' – if anything, it points to the limitations of treating them in so abstract a fashion.

According to Althusser and Balibar, however, the interpretation of individuals as *Träger* is central to the theory of historical materialism, and has universal application. It is Althusser's conclusion, in fact, that the object of Marx's study – the 'mechanism of the production of the society effect' – is only complete when

all the effects of the mechanism have been expounded down to the point where they are produced in the form of the very effects that constitute the concrete, conscious or unconscious, relations of individuals to the society as a society, i.e. down to the effects . . . in which men consciously or unconsciously live their lives, their projects, their attitudes and their functions as social. (*RC*, p. 66)

Balibar is no less impressed by the explanatory power of the *Träger* concept, which, he argues, provides the key to a Marxist 'theory of the individual':

We can say that each relatively autonomous practice thus engenders forms of historical individuality which are peculiar to it. This observation results in a complete transformation in the meaning of the term 'men'; which, as we have seen, the Preface to *A Contribution* made the support of the whole construction. We can now say that these 'men', in their theoretical status, are not *the concrete men*, the men, of whom we are told in famous quotations no more than that they 'make history'. For each practice, and for each transformation of that practice, they are the forms of individuality which can be defined on the basis of its combination structure. (*RC*, p. 252)

What is objectionable here is not the suggestion that 'concrete individuals' cannot be the object of a theory, but the implication that 'forms of individuality' can be theorized without reference to the specific effectivity exerted by individuals as unique centres of experience. No doubt, theories, since they have general application, are incapable of 'explaining' the uniqueness of the individual. On this point, indeed, humanist and anti-humanist may agree. The real problem lies not in the assertion of the structured nature of experience, but in the conceptualization of individuals as no more than social 'effects'. For if we play no part in the formation of the structures that dominate us, what sense is there in trying to alter them? If, moreover, the experience of individual men and women is viewed as inessential to their existence, then the category of the 'concrete individual' ceases to have any reference to *human* beings; within the confines of such a theory, one can no longer speak of individuals as 'dominated' by social structures or in need of 'liberation' from them, since they are not thought of as beings with 'interests' to be affected.

If this is a correct interpretation of the anti-humanism of *Reading Capital*, then Althusser and Balibar are guilty of a fraudulent reading of Marx. Some have claimed, however, that if the more extreme formulations of *Reading Capital* are discarded, its anti-humanist argument can still be defended. John Mepham has argued, for example, that there are two distinct 'anti-humanist formulae' in Althusser's work, one unacceptably extreme (the *Träger* formula), the other correct.[14]

This moderate anti-humanist does not deny the effectivity of human subjects, but only their effectivity as individuals. It is an attack on the false identification of individuals as the subjects of the historical process – an identification supposedly implied by all 'humanist' formulae to the effect that 'men' ('men and women') make history. It is a demand that we replace such formulae by others which express the truth that history is the product not of individuals but of mass action. 'It is the masses which make history. The class struggle is the motor of history. . . .'[15]

Why this insistence upon the displacement of the category of 'men'? The answer, apparently, is that 'humanist' talk reinforces the powerlessness of the worker:

> If the workers are told that 'it is men who make history' that helps to disarm them. It tends to make them think that they are all-powerful as men, whereas they are disarmed as workers in the face of the power which is really in common: that of the bourgeoisie, which controls the *material* and *political* conditions determining history. The humanist line turns them away from class-struggle, prevents them making use of the only power they possess: that of their organisation as a class by means of their class organisations (the trade union, the party).[16]

With this claim (whose truth can only be established empirically), the debate shifts on to the ground of tactics rather than philosophy; but even here the 'humanist' might well have the better case, for to convince workers of their impotence scarcely seems the best way of persuading them to participate in collective action. There seems, in any case, something fundamentally ill-conceived about this line of defence; for if Althusserianism does indeed amount to no more than a reminder that it is collective rather than individual action that 'makes history', then we have been given no reason in theory to suppose it incompatible with Sartre's argument in the *Critique of Dialectical Reason*. Of course, it is always possible that what we call 'Althusserianism' is not a distinctive theory at all, but a theoretical journey that sets out from radical structuralism to find itself returning, by way of various self-criticisms, to the Sartrean Marxism that it originally felt so confident of refuting. In this event 'moderate' anti-humanism may in reality be a thinly veiled humanism.

In any case, *Reading Capital* cannot be invoked in support of the idea that 'classes' make history, since it argues quite explicitly that classes themselves are '*Träger*' of social relations: 'the definition of the social relations of production implies a "support" function defined as a class' (*RC*, pp. 233 and 267). The edifice is ingenious: individuals and classes are *Träger* of social relations; but what are social relations? John Mepham has certainly seen the risk in this runaway use of the *Träger* formula, arguing that it must not be interpreted in a manner incompatible with the fact that 'human social relations are only possible because they involve . . . men and not, say, rocks or dogs'.[17] According to Mepham, however, Althusser's fault is that he neglected the possibility of supplementing the 'science of social formations' by other disciplines, rather than that he excluded these. This is hard to reconcile either with Althusser's claims about the 'mythical' status of any anthropology,[18] or with his criterion of 'scientificity', for he would be bound to reject such disciplines were they to attribute any explanatory status to subjective states or attitudes, or conscious decisions. Surely Althusser's conception of science is already cast in the mould of an *a priori* anti-humanism?

Althusser tells us in his *Essays in Self-Criticism* that he never wanted to be interpreted as denying the existence of human beings. Hence his impatience with the charge of some of his critics that his theory 'eliminates' men and women; and his insistence that Marx's constant use of the concepts of 'place' and 'function' and of '*Träger*' was not intended to evacuate the concrete realities – 'to reduce real men to pure functions of support' – but to render mechanisms intelligible by grasping them in their concept, and on that basis to render intelligible the concrete relations which cannot be grasped except via the 'detour' of abstraction (*SC*, p. 130).

Now this seems to suggest that the humanist and anti-humanist positions are compatible in the sense that the real nature of individuals is not in question: only 'abstractly' are they 'supports', concretely they are the rational and moral beings the humanist supposes them to be. Why then must they relate to themselves as '*Träger*' and not as 'making history'? We have already discounted as incoherent the idea that Althusser could want to explain this in terms of our reactions to a certain style of address. Yet, inasmuch as he suggests that reality is unaffected by the concepts employed in its understanding, the answer to this question remains obscure.

One is reminded here of the debate in analytical philosophy between Ayer and Austin over the language of sense-data. When Ayer attempts to defend the sense-datum language as no more than an alternative way of talking about material objects, Austin challenges him to explain why it is so important to use this 'alternative' discourse – and goes on to suggest that what we must detect beneath this supposedly 'neutral' language is Ayer's tacit support for a definite (Berkeleyan) ontological position.

Some similar reluctance to make explicit the rationale for using the *Träger* formula is detectable in Althusser's attempts to defend its utility. The point is highlighted by E. P. Thompson's 'Althusserian' translation:

Let us suppose, at a certain conjuncture, there is a moment within the society effect which 'gives' itself to 'history's' naked eye with the false obviousness of a shop steward saying to his fellow-workers: 'Hey lads! The production manager is coming to the canteen today to give us a pep talk on measured day work. Let's give him a hot reception!' In order to demystify these sentences, and *construct* them, within theory, as rigorous concepts, we must verbalise them thus: 'O *Träger* of proletarian productive relations! The *Träger* allotted a dominant function within bourgeois productive relations will manifest itself in the "Canteen" at this relatively overdetermined conjuncture through the mechanisms of a relatively autonomous ethical effect determined in the last instance by the law of motion of capitalist production relations at the level of the intensified extraction of surplus-value from the labour-power of the proletarian

Träger. It is determined that the conjuncture shall manifest itself in the form of a "hot" contradiction.'[20]

If this kind of clarification can detonate the capitalist order, then why, asks Thompson, have the Althusserians not long ago hurried down to Dagenham or Longbridge?

Thompson's parody touches to the heart of the dilemma of Althusserianism: either, despite his professions to the contrary, we take Althusser to be claiming that we are really no more than *Träger* – in which case there would seem no reason to tell us so, and Althusserian theory has no necessary relevance politically, or we take Althusser at his word, accepting that in our reality we are not pure functions of support – in which case we may be the kind of beings for whom Althusserianism could have political relevance, but we are not really the *Träger* as which we feature in theory.

The dilemma here can be related to the fact that Althusser rejects a simple structuralism while denying the constitutive role of the subject. Althusser recognizes that the existence of a social role to be performed does not itself guarantee there is a subject equipped to perform it, and that it is mistaken to suppose that one can deduce the experience and consciousness of human subjects from the social functions they happen to perform. On these grounds, he rejects the 'pure' structuralist account in terms of the 'essence' of the economy directly generating its 'appearance' in human experience, and argues for the mediating role of ideology in the construction of the subject. Subjects of experience, according to Althusser, are products of ideology, but they are 'relatively autonomous' from their conditions of existence because ideology is not a direct representation of those conditions but the reality in which they live their relations to those conditions. The subject, therefore, is not the direct 'effect' of the economy but the 'effect' of ideological relations whose precise function is to constitute subjects of experience appropriate to the needs of the social division of labour and distribution of economic functions. Subjects are 'produced' for the places in society they support.[21]

But unless individuals are to be credited with 'naturally' possessing the capacities enabling them to recognize that which will constitute them as 'subjects' (a position ruled out by Althusser's rejection of a humanist epistemology), then the subject is already presupposed to its formation, and Althusser's argument is circular. Subjects, he says, recognize themselves in ideology. But who does the recognizing if not the subject as conceived within humanism?

British Althusserianism

It is on precisely these grounds that the 'British Althusserians' have taken issue with Althusser, though unlike his other critics they approve his overall theoretical approach. Professing themselves both anti-humanist and Marxist, they differ from Althusser in interpreting Marxism not as a science but as a 'political theory' or 'medium of political calculation',[22] constructing political situations by providing 'objectives' for action and 'discursive means for characterizing the situation of action' (i.e. ways of talking about what is to be done).

While applauding Althusser for his attempt to escape the classic subject–object epistemology, in which subjects are viewed as centres of cognition of a reality which is 'represented' to them in consciousness, Paul Hirst has complained that his theory of ideology is inadequate to the task, since it presupposes a (humanist) 'founding' subject as a condition of the functioning of the mechanism whereby 'subjects' are constituted as 'effects'. In the first instance, Hirst argues, ideology is said to constitute concrete individuals (not-yet-subjects) as subjects. Such a theory, however, presupposes that concrete individuals possess the faculties requisite to their becoming subjects. In an attempt to avoid this circularity, Althusser then supposes that subjects are 'always already' subjects, and concrete individuals only abstract relative to the ideological individuals (i.e. constituted subjects) which they 'really' are. But 'unless we fill the child's cradle with anthropological assumptions'[23] – which would, of course, imply a disastrous lapse into humanism – there is nothing, says Hirst, to guarantee that the infant (or adult) 'subject' will recognize itself in the mirror of Ideology as the kind of subject it is supposed to be (or become). Once again, therefore, the subject is presupposed as a subject internal to the specular structure, a structure which is thus revealed to be, in reality, none other than the reviled structure of empiricism–idealism:

> The subject which the individual is to be represents the essence, an essence which transcends the 'abstract' individual, and the 'abstract' individual represents the 'subject', an empty individual with nothing but the faculties necessary to receive the subject that it will be.[24]

As we have already seen, what this conclusion suggests, of course, is that a 'pure' anti-humanism is incompatible with the construction of a social theory such as Marxism.

Hirst proposes, therefore, to cut the tenuous link between Althusserian Marxism and human experience. The resulting theory is constructed around two theses, the first of which amounts to a denial that it is meaningful to speak of 'human subjects' at all. The evidence for this claim is said to lie in psychoanalysis: since Freud's paper on the Unconscious, we have had to accept that we are profoundly mistaken in thinking of ourselves as a 'unity of consciousness'. Hence it is possible, indeed necessary, to think of human individuals not as 'the unitary terminal of an "imaginary" subject, but as the support of a decentred complex of practices and statuses which have distinct conditions of existence'.[25] However, the experience of the self as a 'unity of consciousness' was not eliminated by Freud's theory of the unconscious; nor did Freud intend it to be. If he had this would make nonsense of the psychoanalyst's attempt to bring individuals to cognition of their unconscious motivations. The process depends on the experience of the self as a conscious unity, and this provides the concept of the 'subject' with its reference. 'Subjects' which are not such unities *are not subjects* – at least, not human subjects.

Hirst's second thesis is that it is mistaken to suppose that ideology represents an independent reality to a subject. The Marxist theory of ideology, together with its reliance, covert or otherwise, on a 'humanist' subject, must therefore be abandoned. According to Hirst, one can speak of means of representation and signifying practices, but not of a reality which they represent. Hence there is no essential unity to the ideological, nor any necessary relationship between it and conditions of human existence: any and every ideology is possible at any time.

Hirst is left in the uncomfortable position of arguing, on the one hand, that ideology does not represent anything, while claiming, on the other, that ideological systems have political significance and consequences. For how can one determine what is 'significant' in that event? And how can one determine the 'consequences' of ideology if it has no necessary bearing on reality? Why, indeed, does it matter what happens to 'subjects' in ideology if they are no more than the supports of the systems which make them who they are? British Althusserianism may achieve the final eradication of the humanist subject, but only at the cost of removing any rational grounds for preferring one social system to another.

The politics of anti-humanism

Althusser presented his attack on the Feuerbachian reading of Marx as an attack upon its *theoretical* inadequacies. He was also convinced, however, that it had damaging political consequences in the form of 'socialist humanism'.

'Socialist humanism' he argues, is an ideological discourse which socialists need in order to 'live' their relations to a definite economic-political 'conjuncture';[26] but it remains attached to a bourgeois problematic, able to reflect but never to grasp in thought the reality which gives rise to it.

As the ideology of Marxism, 'socialist humanism' is a form of misrecognition – an attempt to supply us with a 'human essence' in which we can discover a 'common purpose', a potential for 'authenticity', and certain 'universal interests' (peace, respect for human rights, the dignity of the person, the end of exploitation). But this 'essence' does not exist; it reflects merely the interest of socialism, which discovers it because it needs it. The couple human/inhuman has no absoluteness; it is a formal structure of thought whose content is supplied for each historical epoch by the dominant interests within it:

> Speaking of the idea of man and of humanism in *The German Ideology*, Marx commented that the idea of human nature, or of the essence of man, concealed a *coupled value judgement*, to be precise, the couple human/inhuman; and he wrote: 'The "inhuman" as much as the "human" is a product of present conditions; it is their negative side'. The couple human/inhuman is the hidden principle of all humanism, which is then no more than a way of living-sustaining-resolving this contradiction. Bourgeois humanism made man the principle of all theory. This luminous essence of man was the visible counter-part to a shadowy inhumanity. By this part of shade, the content of the human essence, that apparently absolute essence announced its rebellious birth. The man of freedom-reason denounced the egoistic and divided man of capitalist society. In the two forms of this couple human/inhuman, the bourgeoisie of the eighteenth century lived in 'rational-liberal' form, the German left radical intellectuals in 'communalist' or 'communist' forms, the relations between them and their conditions of existence, as a rejection, a demand and a programme. (*FM*, pp. 236–7)

In the same way 'socialist humanism', according to Althusser, is simply the form in which socialists in the West express their dissent from discrimination and exploitation, and those in the East denounce the 'abuses' of the dictatorship of the proletariat and the 'cult of personality'. Since it remains an ethical, and thus ideological, phenomenon, we must 'go beyond', socialist humanism by means of a scientific analysis of the conjuncture which gives rise to it.[27]

Yet the only 'socialist humanism' which receives serious attention in *For Marx* is that of the USSR. And despite what he says in 'Marxism and Humanism', Althusser does not regard socialist humanism as a necessary ideology of socialism but as a deplorable distortion of it. 'Marxism and Humanism' is an attack on Soviet 'revisionism' conducted from a Maoist point of view. It is presented, however, as if all that were at stake were the possible corruption that the language of 'socialist humanism' might introduce into the otherwise wholly authentic process of socialist construction in the USSR. In fact, under cover of a theory of the necessity of humanist ideology to socialism, Althusser is attacking that construction process itself.

For 'socialist humanism' is, in reality, an irredeemably bourgeois 'individualist' philosophy. Hence, we are led to believe, the fault of the USSR was not that it failed to practise the 'socialist humanism' which it preached (the charge brought against it by so many 'socialist humanists' both East and West), but that it allowed its revolution to be compromised by bourgeois values.

Defending Althusser against the charge of 'Stalinism', Perry Anderson has argued that his attack on socialist humanism must be understood in the light of his sympathy for China.[28] The references to stated Soviet intentions were all intended as sardonic criticisms of the failure of the USSR to implement them in practice. But to reveal Althusser's Chinese leanings is not thereby to exonerate him of 'Stalinism', and if it were true that Althusser was merely attacking the Soviet Union for the hypocrisy of its humanist rhetoric, then he would not have differed from those 'socialist humanists' in the West whom he explicitly criticized for their 'obsession with ethics'.

It is a central theme of anti-humanism that humanist argument rests upon a merely 'moral' or 'ethical' basis, which precludes any genuine theoretical understanding.[29] Since moral discourse fails to direct attention to the underlying forces (economic relations, social institutions, etc.) responsible for the 'effects' it approves or condemns, it must, so it is argued, mislead people as to the true source of their grievances and hence result in wrongly targeted or ineffective political activity.

Now this is a fair enough charge to bring against any current of humanist thought which makes the premise of its 'ethical' approach the false assumption that values are arrived at autonomously of any factual state of affairs. For since affective and moral feeling is an instrinic component of our experience as a whole, it has to be understood as biologically and culturally conditioned. One cannot, therefore, arrive at an adequate comprehension of society if one supposes values to be 'freely chosen' by 'sovereign' individuals, and the anti-humanists are right to reject any 'moralism' based on that approach.

But one must also object to their own tendency to overlook or deny the distinctive character of affective and moral experience. It is just as implausible to suppose that conscious experience is the mere by-product or 'epiphenomenon' of social structures and economic relations as it is to suppose that the latter have no impact upon its formation. Nor is it realistic to treat morality as a form of conspiracy arising with the bourgeois epoch. This is the line adopted by that crude 'Marxism', which would have us identify 'morality' with 'bourgeois values' and view the latter as ideologically 'constructed'. But the suggestion that the moral attitudes suited to the maintenance of capitalism are inculcated into individuals by means of ideological 'apparatuses' must be resisted on several grounds. First, it denies the relative autonomy of moral feeling and action, much of which has little direct political consequence and may even be in conflict with the values dictated by the dominant economic rationality of the day; second, it invites us to view morality as a form of extrinsic repression of our 'natural' selves rather than as an intrinsic form of sensibility essential to any form of human coexistence; and third, it fails to recognize that we must already be creatures possessed of a certain distinctive moral sense if we are to respond to the pressures of 'ideology' in the first place.

If, then, the anti-humanist demand that we dispense with 'ethics' in favour of 'theory' is to be interpreted as a demand that we analyse moral experience as the mere reflex of other, essentially non-moral processes, then it must be rejected. Moral experience requires its own categories and mode of understanding, and cannot be treated as a secondary form of rationality.

Defending moralism against its anti-humanist repudiation, E. P. Thompson has made the point that it is one of the devices of the 'naïve rationalism' of the anti-humanist approach to attempt to 'trick up a new rationalist explanation of non-rational behaviour: that is, affective and moral consciousness must somehow be construed as displaced rationality ("ideology") and not as *lived experience* "handled" in distinctive ways'.[30] This is a valid point. On the other hand, we should note that the anti-humanist can fail to 'handle' moral experience in distinctive ways without denying that it has political effects. So if we want to insist that it matters politically that social theory respects the irreducible nature of 'lived experience', then we must argue that such experience is, within certain limits, self-validating. The humanist, in short, will differ from the anti-humanist, not in defending the idea that moral action is effective, but in defending it as itself a form of truth.

How far this humanist position is Marxist is debatable. Marx, it is true, drew a distinction in *The German Ideology* between consciousness as 'practical experience' and the 'ideological' consciousness which misrecognizes its own relationship to 'reality'; but the difference between the two is neither clearly formulated nor pursued further. In any case, as far as morality is concerned, Marx is decidedly biased towards presenting it as a derived and mystified effect of economic forces. He also, of course, argues that human beings are responsible for the creation of alienated and fetishized systems of thinking which profoundly mislead them as to the true meaning of their experience. One way want to reject the anti-humanist presentation of consciousness as necessarily distorting. But any humanist argument must acknowledge that there is a tension between asserting the validity of conscious experience, on the one hand, and appealing to concepts of 'alienation' or 'fetishism', on the other. For if 'lived experience' offers us a measure of truth, it cannot be theorized as if it proceeded in an entirely alien or mystified mode. We must also, of course, be wary of presenting moral feeling as if its 'truth' were unchallengeable. Morality is itself a site of conflict, and there is nothing about having moral convictions that makes them immune to criticism. Nor should we assume all valuing to be moral – for it is quite possible to promulgate a set of values – religious values, for example – which supposedly override those of morality.

Notes

1 Jacques Lacan, *Ecrits: A Selection*, trans. Alan Sheridan (London 1977), p. 148.

2. Michel Foucault, *The Order of Things* (London 1970), p. 351f.
3. ibid., p. 352 (translation modified).
4. Perry Anderson, *In the Tracks of Historical Materialism* (London 1983), p. 37. In an impressive synoptic survey of the development of French thought over the last two decades in his chapter on 'Structure and Subject', Anderson reveals the essential continuity between structuralism and post-structuralism.
5. In the last chapter of *The Savage Mind* (London 1966), Lévi-Strauss directly engages with Sartre's conception of history as a specific domain of human existence to be comprehended only by means of dialectical reason.
6. On these two methods of escaping history ('from the bottom' and 'by the top') see Lévi-Strauss, *The Savage Mind*, p. 261-2.
7. ibid., p. 269.
8. For the remainder of this chapter, references to these works will be abbreviated as follows: *FM* = *For Marx* (Harmondsworth 1966); *RC* = *Reading Capital* (London 1970); *LP* = *Lenin and Philosophy and other essays* (London 1971); *SC* = *Essays in Self-Criticism* (London 1976).
9. For Althusser's theory of the ideological construction of the subject, see *LP*, pp. 127-86, and the discussion of the second part of this chapter.
10. This is Marx's formulation of the problem in his notes on Mill of 1844 (Karl Marx and Frederick Engels, *Collected Works* (London 1975), vol. 3, p. 212) and the same theme is repeated in the *Grundrisse* in the course of the discussion of the alienation wrought by the money system (see pp. 156-60, and p. 331). See also Roman Rosdolsky, *The Making of Marx's 'Capital'* (London 1977), pp. 123-30 (who argues that this same theory of alienation underlies the later theory of the commodity in *Capital*) and John Mepham's critical comments in his review-article on Rosdolsky, in *Issues in Marxist Philosophy* (Brighton 1969), vol. I, pp. 154-9.
11. Marx, *CW*, vol. 3, p. 212.
12. John Mepham, *Issues in Marxist Philosophy*, pp. 156-7.
13. Marx, Preface to first German edition, *Capital*, vol. I, pp. 20-1.
14. John Mepham, 'Who Makes History?', *Radical Philosophy*, no. 6 (winter 1973).
15. This is Althusser's formulation in his *Essays in Self-Criticism*, p. 46 and p. 51.

16 John Mepham, 'Who Makes History?', p. 23.
17 ibid., pp. 26-7.
18 See *RC*, pp. 160-7.
19 J. L. Austin, *Sense and Sensibilia* (London 1962), pp. 59-61 and pp. 105-7.
20 E. P. Thompson, *The Poverty of Theory* (London 1978), p. 335.
21 See *LP*, 'Ideology and the State', esp. pp. 170-7.
22 Paul Hirst, *Law and Ideology*, p. 3f.
23 ibid., p. 67.
24 ibid., p. 68.
25 ibid., p. 60.
26 'Conjuncture' is defined in the glossary to Althusser's works as 'The central concept of the Marxist science of politics (see also Lenin's ''current moment''); it denotes the exact balance of forces, state of overdetermination of the contradictions at any given moment to which political tactics must be applied.'
27 *FM*, p. 223. The analysis which Althusser proceeds to present should be read in conjunction with that by the socialist humanist, E. P. Thompson, in section xlii of the title essay of *The Poverty of Theory*, pp. 314-34.
28 See Perry Anderson, *Arguments within English Marxism* (London 1980), ch. 4, esp. pp. 107-12.
29 This is a key theme of Anderson's criticism of 'socialist humanist' moralism. 'Did the levy of 1956', he asks (betraying a somewhat biblio-centric conception of history), 'produce a single substantial book, or even analytic essay, on the USSR in the later Khrushchev years?', ibid., p. 119.
30 E. P. Thompson, *The Poverty of Theory*, p. 366.

Further reading

The main source texts for the argument discussed in this chapter are: Claude Lévi-Strauss, *The Savage Mind* (1962) (London 1966); Louis Althusser, *For Marx* (1966), trans. Ben Brewster (Harmondsworth 1969); *Reading Capital* (1968), trans. Ben Brewster (London 1970); *Lenin and Philosophy and other Essays* (writings dating from 1964-70), trans. Ben Brewster (London 1971); *Elements of Self-Criticism* (1974), trans. Grahame Lock (London 1976).

For a short, lucid and very polemical attack on structuralism, see Sebastiano Timpanaro, *On Materialism* (London 1976), pp. 135-58, and Perry Anderson, *In the Tracks of Historical Materialism* (London 1983), pp. 32-55.

For critical commentary on Althusser, see Jacques Rancière, *La Leçon d'Althusser* (Paris 1974) (Rancière's contribution to the original French edition of *Reading Capital* is available in translation as 'The Concept of "Critique" and the "Critique" of Political Economy', *Theoretical Practice*, no. 2 (spring 1971), and is published together with a self-criticism 'How to use *Lire le Capital*', *Economy and Society*, 5 no. 3 (August 1976)); see also Rancière's 'On the Theory of Ideology', *Radical Philosophy*, no. 7 (spring 1974), and Ted Benton, 'Rancière and Ideology', *Radical Philosophy*, no. 9 (winter 1974); André Glucksmann, 'A Ventriloquist Structuralism', *New Left Review*, no. 72 (March-April 1972) (included in *Western Marxism, A Critical Reader* (London 1978) – which is also the source for an interview with Lucio Colletti in the course of which he makes clear his distance from Althusser, see pp. 332-5); Derek Sayer, 'Science as critique: Marx versus Althusser', in *Issues in Marxist Philosophy*, ed. John Mepham and David Hillel Ruben (Brighton 1969), vol. III, pp. 27-54; Norman Geras, 'Althusser's Marxism', *New Left Review*, no. 71 (January-February 1972); Leszek Kolakowski, 'Althusser's Marx', *Socialist Register* (1971); Sebastiano Timpanaro polemicizes with Althusser in *On Materialism*, and extended attacks on Althusserianism are to be found in E. P. Thompson, *The Poverty of Theory* (London 1978), and Simon Clarke, *One Dimensional Marxism* (London 1980). Paul Hirst has criticized Althusser's theory of ideology while remaining convinced of the advance that Althusserianism represents over humanist thinking – see 'Althusser and the theory of ideology', *Economy and Society*, 5 no. 4 (November 1976) (now included with other essays on Althusser in *On Law and Ideology* (London 1979)); see also Paul Hirst and Barry Hindess, *Mode of Production and Social Formation* (London 1977), pp. 28-30. Jorge Larrain, *The Concept of Ideology* (London 1979), offers a number of sympathetic criticisms (see esp., pp. 154-64). For strong criticism of the argument of Hindess and Hirst, see Tony Skillen, 'Post-Marxist Modes of Production', and Andrew Collier, 'In Defence of Epistemology', both in *Radical Philosophy*, no. 20 (summer 1978).

E. P. Thompson's account of experience and agency is critically discussed by Perry Anderson in *Arguments within English Marxism* (London 1980). Argument very relevant to the debate on 'moralism' (though developed primarily in relation to the work of Jürgen Habermas) is to be found in Russell Keat, *The Politics of Social Theory* (Oxford 1981) – see especially his chapter on 'Value-Freedom and Socialist Theory', part IV. Also pertinent are: Brian Fay, *Social Theory and Political Practice* (London 1975); Anthony Giddens, *Positivism and Sociology* (London 1975); and Roy Bhaskar, *The Possibility of Naturalism* (Hassocks 1979) (see in particular his chapter on 'Agency').

6
The subjectification of the subject: Lacan and Foucault

Disillusionment with Marxism

Althusser's attempt to rescue Marxism from the clutches of phenomenology has been an issue of far less importance to the development of French thought over the last decade than the attention paid to Marxist anti-humanism in this country might lead one to expect. For even before Althusser had embarked on his attempt to bring Marxism into line with structuralism, structuralism had moved on through the work of Lacan, Foucault and Derrida to a position which would condemn as itself 'humanist' the commitment to rationality which lies behind all interpretations of Marx, Althusser's included.

From the vantage of the attack that the 'post-structuralists' have mounted on western metaphysics, it is the fundamental Enlightenment underpinning of Marxism that has been called in question and condemned for its anthropocentricism: with or without the trappings of an explicit philosophical anthropology, Marxism is to be regarded as irredeemably 'humanist' because it takes the *unity* of humanity and nature as its starting point. Behind the idea that it is *we* who are in principle the controlling force over our environment and able to act in the light of reason to ensure our progressive emancipation, there lies, so it is claimed, an essentially Hegelian synthesis of the in-itself of nature and the for-itself of humanity.[1] This depicts the 'human' as able to transgress its 'culturality' in an extension of itself with the 'natural', and the 'natural' as engulfed in the 'humanization' of a thought which posits from the outset its identity with the 'human'. It is this humanist premise, it is said, which lies at the very root of Marxism, since from the standpoint of historical materialism it is through human *practice* that things are developed and transformed, and by reference to human needs and goals that the effects of that transformation are measured and assessed.

A 'philosophy of difference', however, resists the synthesizing project of any form of dialectical thinking – regardless of whether the synthesis is viewed, idealistically, as achieved in thought, or, materialistically, as the outcome of practice. On this view, difference must always be maintained, and the radical heterogeneity of all things opposed to the generalizing unifications of the dialectic. Althusser himself must therefore be accounted 'humanist' for privileging human practice, seeing in it the expression of the essence of things in general:

Althusser has still not gone beyond the *humanisation* of the identity between subject and object. . . . Doubtless it is no longer said that the concept conceives of itself, or that it discovers in its conception (or consciousness) of itself the identity of being and concept. But it is freely said that theory, in knowing the essence of theoretical practice (its own essence therefore), knows every practice. Such a 'practice in general' means less the activities indulged in by specimens of the human race on the surface of the earth than an equivalent of the 'unity of man and nature', the noblest designation of the 'totality'. . . .[2]

It would be mistaken to suppose, however, that the 'settling of accounts' with Marxism that proceeded apace after 1968 was inspired by purely metaphysical considerations. For the reaction in the first instance was to Marxism as a political theory and practice. Some of the seeds of the nihilistic, or Rightist, thinking in France in recent years, are to be found, in fact, in the anti-authoritarianism of the rebellion of May 1968 – which called in question both the repressive practice of the *PCF* and the validity of the Marxist analysis of power. Not only did the May protest challenge the standard Marxist account of the genesis and agency of any movement seeking revolutionary change within advanced capitalist society; it also exposed in the starkest possible manner how inflexible and dogmatic the attitude of the official communists really were – since, rather than offer an analysis of the 'concrete conjuncture' in all its contradictory aspects, they preferred to cling to the shibboleths of Marxist doctrine and to force events to conform to their 'truth'. (Althusser, for example, analysed the 'conjuncture' as a workers' strike 'preceded' and 'accompanied' by an *ideological* revolt on the part of the students and petty bourgeois individuals[3] – in other words, discovered in it a classic conflict between proletariat and ruling class.) But perhaps most importantly, both in what it achieved and in its failure, the May movement indicated the need for a reappraisal of the nature and operation of power in modern industrial societies. In its success, it revealed the vulnerability of the forces of 'law and order' to styles of protest that broke with the traditions of Left militancy. ('The authorities', it has been said, 'could successfully oppose a *coup d'état* such as the putsche in Algiers in 1961, but not a carnival'.)[4] In its failure, it suggested the weakness of any analysis of power based on the idea of a centralized State authority which protects the interests of a ruling élite against the demands of a unified opposition. It thereby also raised the question of the complicity of the oppressed in their own oppression: if the carnival spirit proved unsustainable, how far did that bespeak a limitation on the tolerance of the anarchic and libertarian forces it set in motion, a resistance of the 'enslaved' to their own emancipation?

The new orientations in French philosophy – and the general shift in emphasis from the work of Marx to that of Nietzsche which they represent – have therefore involved more than a general challenge to reason in itself. Foucault, for example, has argued for the intimate link between knowledge and power, Deleuze for the existence of a 'desire' which remains authentic only in so far as it is prior to any order or systematization, Lacan for the inevitability of our 'subjection', and Derrida for the 'originary difference' which frustrates every attempt at unity. The political message, therefore, tends to pessimism, emphasizing the obstacles presented by language or by the psyche itself to the remaking of social institutions.

Where the humanist sees a confrontation between agents possessed of will and reason and the 'unwilled' and 'irrational' products of their concerted actions, the anti-humanist views the wills themselves as 'unwilled' and the 'reason' in whose name every 'progress' is supposedly made as no more obviously to be privileged than the 'madness' it opposes. Lacan, it is true, had reasserted the claims to attention of the human subject against its elimination in structuralism proper. But his call for a 'return to Freud' was made not in order to resurrect the conscious subject of experience, but to convince us of the illusory identity of the ego. Since the Lacanian account implies that the forces responsible for the construction of identity are necessarily beyond the control of those they constitute, it directly challenges the premises traditionally invoked in support of the possibility of social progress.

It is difficult, in fact, to see how the political outlook of the structuralist movement could be other than 'pessimistic', since it condemns as 'humanist mythology' the very mode of thinking that conceives of history as 'progress'. Indeed, if it is mistaken to want to assess the course of history in humanist terms, then it becomes absurd to attempt to evaluate historical outcomes at all; history is simply a series of occurrences without end or meaning. In that sense it is only from humanist premises than one can apply the labels 'nihilist', 'pessimist' and the like to the anti-humanist camp. As we shall see, however, those defending anti-humanist positions are themselves quite ready to employ a rhetoric of 'loss', 'lack', 'subjection' and 'repression' suspiciously akin to that of traditional humanism.

Anti-humanism and linguistics

The structuralist/post-structuralist movement came into being through what has been called an 'exorbitation of language',[5] and in almost all its theoretical moves has referred, if not deferred, to the account of language provided by Ferdinand de Saussure.

According to Saussure, the sign is not the connection of a name and a thing, but a 'mysterious union' of a sound (acoustic image) and a thought (concept), both of which are in principle exchangeable for other sounds or concepts. Signs are significant in virtue of the total system in which they function, and this is true both at the level of the acoustic image (where it is not the sound that matters but the phonic differences which allow a word to be distinguished from others), and at the level of the concept (for that, too, is defined by its differential relations with other concepts).

While this certainly indicates that the value of a sign is to be understood as a twofold affair, i.e. we have to know not only its relations with other words in the same code for which it can be substituted, but also the idea or concept for which it is exchangeable, it is none the less clear that by privileging relations between terms in one category (the signifier) or the other (the signified) one is invited to conceive of two quite separate orders closed in upon themselves. In other words, one is led to disregard the question of the relationship of language to the world, and to consider the sign system as shut in upon itself.

Saussure himself, when he stresses the purely relational nature of the linguistic system, implies that it is mistaken in principle to search for an 'exit' from it. We should not, he argues, think of signs as pre-existing the relations between them, but as themselves the effects of the play of differences. But Saussure also recognizes, of course, that the purpose of a signifier is to signify: signs only exist (as do the differences between them) in order to communicate meanings. It is only if there is access to the signified that it is possible to distinguish between signs.

It is, however, precisely this necessary but 'false' gesturing of the sign to a concept 'signified in and of itself' that provokes Derrida's polemic with the sign as an unconscious carrier of 'logocentric metaphysics' (i.e. of the philosophical quest for an origin or foundation in truth, reason or the *logos*'). Saussure's analysis of the sign shows it to be 'present' only in its relations with other 'absent' signs, hence never really present; and yet in recognizing the subordination of the signifier to its signified, Saussure must, inconsistently, allow the sign to have reference to an 'immediate presence of thought' outside the play of difference. Saussurean linguistic theory, suggests Derrida, tends in consequence to a 'logocentric' and expressivist view of language as conveying a meaning 'given' to the speaker prior to speech, and in that sense independently of it. Moreover, in committing this inevitable 'error', Saussure necessarily commits another: that of 'phonocentrism' – the unjustifiable view that speech lies at the origin of writing and has, relative to it, a privileged access to meaning.[6]

Even structuralist linguistics, then, in retaining a reference to the 'original' thought which the speaker expresses (either 'immediately' in speech or in 'secondary' fashion by means of writing) contains a 'humanist' bias according to Derrida. But Saussure himself places 'antihumanist' emphasis on the subordination of the individual to the code. Linguistic study, he tells us, must abstract from the physical, physiological and psychological aspects of language in order to concentrate upon '*langue*' as 'a self-contained whole'.[7] And to this we can expect the 'humanist' to object along one or another of two opposing lines. The 'spiritualist' objection would be that Saussure denies individual linguistic creativity; the 'materialist' would criticize its tendency to sever language from its anchorage in the 'natural' world as studied in human biology.[8]

An even more extreme bias against the 'subject' is to be found in formalized structuralist linguistics – which has gone beyond the idea of language as a socially instituted system of rules to which the individual must accommodate as a condition of communication, to argue the purely functional (support/ *Träger*) role of the language users: everything is already 'within' language, and the notion of a signifier distinct from a signified becomes suspect.

Needless to say, both poles of the humanist criticism of structuralist linguistics apply with even greater force to such formalism. The 'spiritualist' will object that human creativity is now not merely excluded from study but actually denied; the materialist, that its account is wholly idealist.[9]

Jacques Lacan: psychoanalysis is not a psychologism

The application of structural linguistics to other regions of study has nowhere proved more decisive for the discipline in question, nor bred more controversy, than in the case of Jacques Lacan's linguistic reformulation of Freudian theory. It may seem paradoxical that it is precisely in the domain of psychology, to which traditionally psychoanalysis has been assigned, that the category of the 'subject' should find itself so beseiged by anti-humanist forces; and to those who are, to say the least, sceptical of the legitimacy of any extension of the theory of language beyond its particular region of study, Lacan's emplanting of the banner of the sign upon the territory where the human subject might be deemed most sovereign – the site of the mind itself – will seem the most arrogant of imperialisms.

Yet the defendants of Lacan's 'return' to Freud will insist that he has done no more than what Freud himself warranted, namely to register the rupture of psychoanalysis with every psychology based on humanist categories. What Freud established, so it is claimed, is the falsity of psychologism in the study of the psyche. According to Lacan, what Freud shows is that an individual is not born human but only becomes so through incorporation into a cultural order. Hence psychology's true object is not the 'nature' of an (already) human mind, but its 'becoming-human' – the process whereby animals of a certain kind become human subjects. Specifically human subjectivity comes into being through subjection to what Lacan terms the Symbolic Order, the order of 'Otherness', in which we can distinguish ourselves from others and refer to ourselves as 'I'.

Access to the Symbolic Order is only given in language, but it proceeds by way of a 'mirror stage', in which the child assumes itself to be the 'other' it sees reflected, and models itself upon its image. At this

'Imaginary' stage of psychic development, the distinction – which only language enables us to make – between self and other, self and the world, is not established. Language, therefore, according to Lacan, imposes order on our otherwise inchoate desire, or rather, since desire is essentially desire of the Other, and the Other is differentiated only in so far as it is signified, the Symbolic Order brings desire into being. In this sense, what is desired is submission to the Symbolic Law. There is, none the less, something prior to the Symbolic Order which 'submits', and which is sacrified to its signifier when it attains existence in language. This sacrifice, moreover, leaves its scars – the series of 'effects' known as the Unconscious. <u>The Unconscious, Lacan tells us, is nothing other than a language, a chain of signifiers of a 'repressed' desire that remains only in so far as it is signified.</u>

It is central to Lacan's argument that Saussure's distinction between signifier and signified marks an unbridgeable gulf. Since psychoanalysis is concerned with a conscious discourse whose signification is never what it means but always 'overdetermined' (a condensation or displacement of what it 'truly' signifies), it follows that the Unconscious is only accessible in language. The most the analyst can do, therefore, is to embark on a decoding of the conscious statements of the patient. But since one can never decode except into the signifying chain, in which any discovered meaning must always inhere and find expression, so the signified of unconscious discourse remains in principle unattainable. The truth of the repression is lost to both patient and analyst alike; in its pre-signified existence, it resides in a different dimension which is inaccessible to language and symbolization – the dimension Lacan refers to as the 'Real'.

It follows that it is impossible to express that which gives rise to subjectivity. Conscious discourse is always the effect of a meaning beyond the reach of the speaking subject: ' "It" (the Id) thinks in a place where it is impossible to say "I am" .' It is in the light of this anti-humanist presentation of the conscious subject as a series of effects arrived at autonomously of the mind itself, that we have to understand Lacan's relentless attack on any theorization of psychoanalysis that reduces it to a psychology centred on a supposedly irreducible subject, whether conceived in behaviourist or existentialist terms. Freud's 'Copernican revolution', according to Lacan, consisted of showing the identity of the ego to be a fictional device covering over the child's loss or sacrifice of an unsignified desire.

Since, according to Lacan, the 'Phallus' is the central organizing signifier of human culture, one's identity, or place in culture, is inevitably allotted by a 'Law of the Father'. Regardless of the actual nature of relations between parent and child, the possibilities and limitations of the latter's passage into adulthood (and specifically upon the acquisition of sexual identity), are determined by the patriarchal ordering of culture. Failure to negotiate a successful entrance into that order results in madness; sanity, on the other hand, is purchased only at the cost of a certain organization of desire (the repression of all desire proscribed by the law of incest) and is the mark of our conformity to the 'desires' of a culture which impoverishes desire in so far as it will only permit a single representative of sexual difference – the anatomical difference between men and women. Anatomical difference comes to feature as the sole index of sexual difference, thus covering over the complexity of the child's early sexual life by a simple opposition.[10]

Lacan's insistence upon the cultural construction of gender difference has recommended his thought to feminists. It none the less begs a crucial question: why is the Phallus the privileged signifier? Lacan cannot attribute its predominance to any feature that the child distinguishes pre-symbolically, since on his own account no differentiation is possible at that level. But the subordination of the female is equally presupposed, and therefore not explained, if Lacan relies (as at one stage of his thinking he appears to) on Lévi-Strauss's notion of kinship in which women are defined as objects of exchange. In both explanations, in fact, language is viewed as the mere mediator of an already, socially, humanly, instituted order, rather than the founding moment of that order.

It has been suggested that in his later work Lacan comes to regard language as the source and purveyor of a mythology of sexual identity and relationship. The meanings introduced in symbolization do not reflect pre-existing values, but make up for their absence.[11] But this offers no solution to the question of masculine privilege, since it remains to ask why it is that women feature in this construction as those who are excluded and defined as *negation* of the male; nor does it explain the urge to 'compensate' for an absence of sexual relationship. What it does imply, of course, is that we should replace the idea that human culture mediates a natural difference between the sexes, by a conception of it as constructing difference: within this construction, woman is 'object', man is 'subject', but both are only 'subjects' by virtue of their reliance upon that order and therefore through subjection to it. Against the idea of natural heterogeneity and its supposition of a primordial biological determination of what is possible for human beings in the way of 'living' their sexuality and 'having' sexual relations, Lacan suggests that both sexes are equally victims, or carriers, of a shared mythology. This position would appear to rule out as 'impossible' any feminism based on a 'return' to a primary feminity, an 'essence' of woman outside 'male-dominated' language. If the feminine is constructed within language, then there is no escape to its 'truth' outside language, no restitution of the feminine in the maternal body or distinctively female drive.

If there is no prediscursive reality to which women (or men) can turn in the struggle against a patriarchal ordering of society, then the challenge to the phallic status can only be made in language. But this implies nothing less than the construction of a different logic, since it would mean refusing the Symbolic Order which alone secures subjectivity. In other words, not only is the whole of humanity implicated in any attempt to dismantle patriarchy, but the whole of humanity would be thrown into an identity crisis. Lacan frees us from the materialist constraints of biology only by tightening the grip of ideas. Since one can only refuse the Symbolic Order from the standpoint of an identity acquired within it, one is eternally trapped by the fact that the structures under attack are essential to formulating any challenge to them. This is the impasse of the Lacanian position: backing up against a 'humanist' reminder of the indispensability of 'being a subject' to being human, there is the 'anti-humanist' insistence upon the alien, because symbolically constructed nature, of the self.

At the same time, Lacan's theory exemplifies the tendency of anti-humanist argument to secrete humanist rhetoric. For where, if not from humanist sources, does the language of struggle, victimization and loss originate? In this connection, we might note that Althusser, while enthusing over the manner in which Lacan has rescued Freud once and for all from the distortion of humanist readings, himself offers a paraphrase of Lacanianism which verges on melodrama. The concern of psychoanalysis, he tells us, is a 'war': a war 'declared in each of its sons, who projected, deformed and rejected, are required, each by himself in solitude and against death, to take the long forced march which makes a mammiferous larvae into human children, *masculine* or *feminine* subjects'.[12] Ambushed even 'before his first cry' by the remorseless Law of Culture and the discourse of 'the Great Third', the infant has no choice but to submit to the 'imposition, imposture, complicity and denegation of its own imaginary fascinations'.[13] But by reference to what, if not to that which is explicitly denied, the preconstituted 'humanity' of these 'mammiferous larvae', is one invited to regret and deplore the tragedy of their humanization? From where, if not from some humanist vantage point, does Althusser discover so tragic a destiny for humankind in the inexorable nature of its cultural rule?

It may be said that Althusser is not so much rebelling against cultural oppression as taking masochistic delight in the crushing blows it delivers. But, in any case, how immutable is the Law of the Father? The force of this question is bound to strike one when Althusser produces such banalities as the following:

That in the Oedipal phase the sexed child becomes a sexual human child (man or woman) by testing its imaginary phantasms against the Symbolic, and if all 'goes well' finally becomes and accepts itself as what it is: a little boy or little girl among adults, with the rights of a child in this adult world, and, like all children with the full *right* to become one day 'like daddy', i.e. a masculine human being with a wife (and no longer only a mother); or 'like mummy', i.e. a feminine human being with a husband (and not just a father) – these things are only the destination of the long forced march towards human childhood.[14]

For without denying that culture is patriarchal and looks like remaining so for a good while yet, one must surely question the relevance of this 'Janet and John' Lacanianism in the context of changing attitudes to gender and parenthood.

The Phallus, according to Lacan, determines the forms in which it may be resisted. But does this mean that patriarchy is insurmountable? Is no point ever reached when the empirical changes brought about by resistance to patriarchy amount themselves to its overthrow? For the theorist to continue indefinitely to see the mark of a predetermining 'law' on every social development which challenges its rule seems pedantic at best.

We can well imagine a future in which the Lacanian conception of the self has become part of common sense itself, part of any subject's consciousness of self. But since, according to that very conception, the self-aware self is a misrecognizing self, the self aware of its self-awareness is itself misrecognizing itself . . . *ad infinitum*. In what sense, then, does Lacanian theory lay claim to have discovered any important truths about psychology? The 'I' which analyses the perfidy of the 'I' must itself be a traitor to the truth. It has been suggested, that we must understand Lacan as speaking the language of the Unconscious itself – as if he were a kind of oracle placed at its disposal. But how can this be when it is the character of unconscious pronouncements to be non-reflexive? If the Unconscious cannot think itself, how can it reproduce itself? That which 'lends' itself to the Unconscious and attempts to speak only its discourse, is, inspite of itself, a conscious 'I', a deliberating ego – and thus, according to Lacan condemned to strive forever too industriously after a truth it can never attain.

The 'philosophy of desire' and the 'New Philosophers'

In the wake of the eruption of a spontaneous desire for liberation that the May 1968 events appeared to manifest, an attempt was made by the so-called 'philosophers of desire' to demolish the Lacanian assumption that since desire was culturally constituted, there was no 'natural' impulse requiring 'liberation' from the impositions of cultural law. The most influential of these challenges to Lacan was the *Anti-Oedipe*, written by Giles Deleuze in collaboration with the Lacanian analyst, Félix Guattari, and published in 1972.[15] According to the *Anti-Oedipe*, social structures 'territorialize' desire in such a manner that it turns reactively against itself. In this perversion of our natural (though unconscious and pre-individual) desire, the Oedipus Complex plays a key role, since in convincing desire of its Oedipal guilt, it teaches it to desire its own repression. Just as Marxists conceive of the capitalist economy as dependent on its 'misrepresentation' in ideology, so Deleuze and Guattari see an 'infrastructural' desire finding expression only in the mystified form of reactive resistance to it. Though the *Anti-Oedipe* is presented as a Freudo-Marxist synthesis, it is more Nietzschean than Freudian in approach, and scarcely very Marxist in its political message. History, it implies, is not so much a struggle of classes as a struggle by the enslaved for their own servitude. Socialism, with its puritanical and authoritarian re-territorializations of desire is to be more feared than capitalism – whose bold and cynical destruction of all ties of family and community releases the individual from the shackling ritual and codification of a collective existence. The affirmative, non-rancorous nature of 'pure' desire is, moreover, directly associated by Deleuze with the noble strength of the

Master class: the exploited are characterized by the force of their desire for weakness, they act not from self-assertion but from resentment-negation of the other, 'the dialectic' being the 'ideology' of this resentment.[16]

But to assert the liberating power of a 'natural' desire which is not socially satisfiable – since it is opposed to the imposition of all form, order and organization – is not in the end to hold out any promise of freedom, but rather to deny its possibility. As Peter Dews has pointed out, 'the *Anti-Oedipe* pays for the "radicality" of its challenge to social institutions with an almost total vacuousness', and in its failure to be able finally to distinguish the 'good' desire from its socially corrupted manifestation 'flips over in a radical pessimism'.[17]

These nihilistic and anti-socialist themes permeate the work of the 'New Philosophers', a rather heterogeneous group of thinkers who gathered in the late 1970s around Bernard-Henri Lévy, an editor with the Grasset publishing house. While presenting themselves as left-wing guardians of the spirit of May 1968 (in which most of them had been active), the New Philosophers found little or nothing worth salvaging from 'socialism' – which they unqualifiedly identified with the practice of the USSR – and readily lent themselves to the, quite predictable, exploitation of their views by the right-wing press.

To some, in fact, it might have seemed that here was a group of left-wing intellectuals prepared to face up fairly and squarely to the evils that could be perpetrated in the name of 'socialism'. Yet in the end their assault upon Marxism (which owed a good deal to the inspiration of Solzhenitsyn) was too sweeping and general to be capable of the discrimination between socialism and its abuse that was essential to any genuine critique of Stalinism. On the other hand, their interest did not really lie in such distinctions, since it was their conviction that the entire framework of Marxist thinking had to be overthrown as insensitive to and oppressive of the libertarianism that had motivated the events of May 1968. It was only, in fact, in so far as it had shown that anti-capitalist protest could wrestle free of the strait-jacket of socialist analysis that the spirit of 1968 was worth preserving.

In the works of some of the New Philosophers (Lardeau and Jambet, Clavel), this spirit is extolled as a quasi-religious experience; in the more secular accounts of Lévy and André Glucksmann, the message is more straightforwardly anarchist, yet at the same time pessimistic, since the stress falls on the fantastic and 'impossible' nature of 1968. The events of May thus come to be seen, not as heralding a possible future, but as a celebration of the unattainable.[18] In a sense, indeed, Marxism had proved profoundly true: the Gulag was not a distortion of it, but a product of its logic. What Marxism had shown was that domination was in fact inevitable and that all efforts to oppose oppression were bound to issue in further servitude. Those who attempted to challenge contemporary forms of power by means of socialist argument, therefore, were only implicating themselves further in the 'domination of theory'. The only viable refuge was to a form of Stoicism, to a private but honourable endurance of one's moral rebellion and despair.

In many respects, the New Philosophers represent a 'humanist' reaction to Marxist authoritarianism. Yet at the same time, distrust of reason and of every form of Enlightenment optimism pervades their writing. Launched in defence of the spontaneous activism of the May events, the 'New Philosophy' comes in the end to advocate a total disengagement from political action: if we would preserve intact our spirit of defiance, then we must renounce politics in favour of the cultivation of an 'inner self'.

Michel Foucault: power, knowledge and individualization

The 'philosophers of desire' had responded to the failure of the classical structuralist argument to offer any basis for a critique of society, by affirming a natural impulse for liberation prior to the imposition of cultural norms and radically repressed by them. But they, too, came to treat desire as self-repressive – an argument forced upon them by their failure to develop any account of the nature and exercise of the power which enforces the containment and perversion of libidinal energy. Just as a theory of power requires a theory of that which is maintained by it or resistant to it, so a theory of desire requires a theory of the power which either represses or promotes its expression.

If we place it in the context of this complementarity of theories of power and theories of desires,[19] then Foucault's work in the 1970s appears as a 'power' rather than 'desire' orientated reaction to the inadequacies made manifest in the structuralist position by the events of May 1968. Even his more structuralist studies of the 1960s, however, anticipate the later focus on the 'economy of power' and on the forms of political rationality embedded in the modern 'welfare' society, in the emphasis they place on the disciplinary control over the community afforded by modern medical and psychiatric techniques. In this sense, the May events served to make more immediate and explicit the concern with power implicit in the earlier studies.

Foucault's work cuts a unique swathe between traditional academic disciplines, but there is one figure – that of Nietzsche – whose influence he fully acknowledges, and one methodological standpoint – that of anti-subjectivism – which has been central to it. The rejection of all anthropological categories and of any reference to a founding 'subject' goes together with a genealogy of reason and madness whose aim is very similar to that which guided Nietzsche's excavations of the origin of good and evil. Just as Nietzsche sought to question the soundness of western morality, so Foucault has aimed to expose the less than wholesome basis of our rationality – and thereby to disturb the complacency with which 'we' humans, joined in reason though divided by time, have passed from century to century the torch of a 'common' sense. And while Nietzsche invoked a 'Will to Power' in order to explain a 'progress' in values which he systematically relativized, and therefore deprived of any goal, so Foucault invokes a 'Will to Truth' as the impulse behind an indefinite accumulation of 'discourses' (or 'knowledges') without apparent purpose.

Noting their similarity in project, Alan Sheridan has suggested that Foucault supplies Nietzsche with the systematic analysis that his thought required but always lacked.[20] Certainly, one way of looking at Foucault is in terms of his taking up the hypothesis of Nietzsche's off-the-cuff remark in the *Genealogy of Morals* that those 'hard atheists', the scientists, are 'not really atheists at all because they still believe in truth', putting it to various 'tests' via the examination of the history of psychopathology, penology, or sexuality, and finding it well-substantiated. In line with Nietzsche's claim that 'reason', 'morality', 'spirit', 'ego', 'motivation' are so many God-surrogates that philosophy inserts into the thinking of European civilization, Foucault denounces the 'humanism' of any account of science/knowledge that still retains this touching faith in truth. We must reject, he says, those absolute categories of epistemology (truth, certainty) or philosophical anthropology (the 'subject', 'influence', 'tradition', 'class consciousness', etc.) to which the human sciences have appealed so regularly in the past.

In *The Archaeology of Knowledge*, Foucault's 'Discourse on Method', written when he was most sympathetic to structuralism,[21] history is dismissed as 'humanist anthropology' whose only aim is to disguise dispersal as identity. By enabling us to isolate the new against the background of the already known (and thus transfer its merit to subjective categories of 'originality', 'genius', 'collective consciousness' and the like), anthropologized history produces the illusion of a community of meaning. It encourages us to suppose that acts and intentions are explanatory; and it invites everyone to think of themselves as belonging within categories which in fact exclude in order to include. Foucault's polemic, however, is not so much with that liberal humanism which attempts to smother difference within an enveloping 'general will' or 'common interest', and of which, after all, both Marxism and existentialism are critical, but with that excluding collectivity of 'reasonable men', that supposedly all-embracing community of the 'sane'.

Foucault's starting-point, which remains, if not the guiding thread throughout his work a very evident influence upon its course, is a conception of madness as that which reason denies, and whose 'silence' is the other face of an all too voluble rationality. While the history of psychiatry typically presents itself as the successive victory of science over superstition – a victory accompanied by the move from the 'inhumane' and 'barbarous' attitudes of the past to the 'civilized' methods of modern medical treatment – the archaeologist of that history will understand that

it is not the progress of knowledge that discovers 'mental illness' where barbarous humanity had been thought to be up against the diabolical and the demonic; it is rather the appearance of the mad person in his new guise of 'mental patient' that gives rise to a scientific discipline by means of which to treat him.[22]

What matters here is not the reality designated by the term 'mental illness', nor the success or failure of the practices adopted towards it by psychotherapy, nor the sufferings of its victims, but the category of the 'mentally ill'. Mental illness, claims Foucault, is 'constituted by all that is said'. Its archaeologist, therefore, is not interested in 'whether witches were unrecognised and persecuted madmen and madwomen, or whether, at a different period, a mystical or aesthetic experience was not unduly medicalised . . .', but in discovering the rules which enable such questions *to be posed* at one time, *not to be posed* at another, and always within the *same* discourse of psychopathology. The point, in short, is to 'dispense with things' in favour of 'things said' (discourses), to define objects as they emerge in discourse without reference to their foundation in things – and the bulk of Foucault's work, even after he abandoned the commitment to structuralist methodology, has consisted precisely in attempts to bring to light the discourses that have constructed 'insanity', 'criminality', 'delinquency', and 'sexuality', and in doing so, brought into being the knowledge of them.

It is the tendency of these studies – and it emerges clearly in his treatment of political action – to reduce behaviour to what is said, to analyse it always as either a form of speech or its effect. He argues, for example, that if political knowledge is understood as discursive practice

> One would not need to pose the psychological problem of an act of consciousness. . . . The question, for example, would not be to determine from what moment a revolutionary consciousness appears, nor the respective roles of economic conditions and theoretical elucidations in the genesis of consciousness . . . but it would try to explain the formation of a discursive practice and a body of revolutionary knowledge that are expressed in behaviour and strategies, which give rise to a theory of society, and which operate the interference and mutual transformation of that behaviour and those strategies.[23]

Now to analyse a discursive formation is to discover the rules which generate its statements. But where are we to look for these rules once we have excluded the 'regulating' nature of the economy, of existing political theories, of human psychology?

In the concluding pages of *The Archaeology of Knowledge*, Foucault allows his 'humanist' critics to place him in the following dilemma: either he must admit that his methods are no better than any others, or he must claim that they are correct. If the latter, then he is allowing his own discourse to constitute an exception to the rules of discourse for which it argues. Foucault does not try to resolve this dilemma, but seeks instead to imply that the 'humanist' case is emotionally rather than rationally based:

What is that fear which makes you reply in terms of consciousness when someone talks to you about a practice, its conditions, its rules, and its historical transformation? What is that fear which makes you see, beyond all boundaries, ruptures, shifts, the great historico-transcendental destiny of the Occident?[24]

Reserving to himself the authorial right of every script-writer, Foucault at this point silences the humanists, but had they been given their lines they might have gone as follows:

It is a classic move of those who attack others from grounds of whose solidity they are not quite sure, that they depict their opponents as swayed by emotion rather than intellect; it is not, however, fear that moves us, but rather reason that makes it difficult for us to budge. It is not that we lack courage to venture forth from our, admittedly rather less than brilliant, Occidental homeland into your depopulated territory of practices, rules and conditions, but rather that we are reminded that it seems part of the destiny of Western thought itself to take us, every so often, into that region. Those very habits of mind which you invite us to forego, are precisely those which force us to think twice about the wisdom of doing so. You say: give up the appeal to consciousness. We say: we shall do so when you find means to address your request to our unconscious. In the meantime, we believe that the 'destiny' of 'the Occident' will only be changed if men and women are in on the act. Consistent with that belief, we shall continue for the time being to be very wary of this invitation to give up all reference to human agents, and to allow instead the language of rules, practices and conditions to become the *lingua franca* of philosophy's brave new world.

If, however, Foucault fudges the response to the humanist challenge in *The Archaeology of Knowledge*, it is because he is still at the time of its writing held in suspense between the positivism of his previous studies and a disinclination to defend them on that methodological ground. With the development of his theory of power, the implicit critical dimension of his work emerges more clearly, but only at the cost of introducing an increasing tension between its anti-humanism and its normative content.

Discipline and Punish, Foucault's first major work of the 1970s,[25] undoubtedly views the changes in social organization which it investigates (those occurring in the transition from the *ancien régime* to the post-Revolutionary society) as mutations in relations of domination. The work focuses on the contrast between the essentially ritualistic and retributive forms of punishment of the feudal era (Foucault's most dramatic example is the torture and execution of the would-be regicide, Damiens), and the system of surveillance instituted by modern penal methods. While in the first instance an 'anonymous' offender is punished in a reassertion of the *personal* power of the King, in the second, an 'impersonal' bureaucratic machinery disciplines the criminal by means of intensively 'individualizing' techniques of scrutiny and bodily control.

The techniques of the 'disciplining' society are epitomized, according to Foucault, in Bentham's 'Panopticon', a prison design incorporating a central watch-tower from which cells radiate so as to isolate their occupants from each other but permit the guard, who cannot be seen by the prisoners themselves, to observe all their movements. The 'efficiency' of such a system is obvious, since it effectively forces the prisoners to become their own warders.

Foucault can, no doubt, be criticized for paying too little heed to the fact that the plan for the Panopticon was never realized, and in fact widely ridiculed at the time;[26] its main value for Foucault, however, is as a metaphor for the rationality he claims is embedded in the forms of power relations distinctive to modern societies. Highly cost-effective, and constraining its victims by moral pressures rather than by violence, modern power operates, says Foucault, in the form of a 'government of individualization': it uses techniques of scientific and administrative inquisition to regiment individuals, and confine them to a certain identity, by depriving them of all links with others and ties of community: it manipulates the 'right' to individuality by recognizing individuals only in their isolation, and thus by denying them everything which makes them truly individual.[27] The techniques in question are essentially threefold: they are those provided by the human sciences, those of the 'dividing practices' (penology, medicine, psychiatry etc.), and those involved in the construction of 'sexuality' (for even our sexual life, according to Foucault, is produced for us through the normalizing technology of a 'sexual machinery').[28] It is with these three modes of 'objectivization' and their implications for the analysis of power, and specifically of its relation to knowledge, that the bulk of Foucault's work in the 1970s has been concerned.

Since Foucault's account of the 'disciplining' society is clearly critical, even at times forcefully condemnatory, it would appear to require the complement of an 'anthropology' at odds with his rejection of humanist categories. Admittedly, Foucault dismisses the traditional 'juridico-discursive' view of power (common, he says, to both the Lacanian conception of desire as the product of Law, and to those who argue for an 'inner' pre-cultural desire) according to which power is essentially unitary, negative and repressive. Power, he claims, is not so much prohibitive as productive. But what exactly does Foucault mean by power? He acknowledges that one cannot speak of power without reference to the desires affected by it, and argues that it is different from the exercise of mere force in that it acts upon behaviour rather than directly upon bodies. He also insists that 'power is exercised only over free subjects and only insofar as they are free'. (Slavery, for example, is not a power relation since the 'determining factors saturate the whole'.)[29] But it is not clear how far this recognition of the 'externality' of the person, and of the person's resistant 'desire', is compatible with Foucault's explication of the positive dimension of power in terms of its 'production' of the subject. For power operates, according to Foucault, by means of a 'subjectification' of persons, a process which he identifies directly with that of their 'subjection'. 'The central intention of Foucault's work', it has been said, 'is to dissolve the philosophical link – inherited by the Marxist tradition from German Idealism – between consciousness, self-reflection and freedom, and to deny there remains any progressive political potential in the idea of an autonomous subject.'[30] But if this is so – and it seems avowed by Foucault himself when he writes that his 'objective' has not so much been the analysis of power but the creation of 'a history of the different modes by which, in our culture, human beings are made subjects'[31] – then every form of resistance, every 'freedom' which resists and every 'desire' for liberation are themselves the effects of specific techniques of power. To this objection that if one is always 'inside' power there can be no 'escape' from it and thus no genuine resistance to it, Foucault, it would seem, has offered no very satisfactory reply.[32]

Foucault's denial of the autonomy of the subject rules out any appeal to a 'higher', alternative, form of political rationality; it also prevents his grounding his critique of power on 'humanist' categories of 'progress' and 'development'. It is neither a superior nor inferior, but merely a different, rationality that dictates that today's marauder in the Queen's bedroom is referred for psychiatric tests when once he would have been consigned to Damiens's terrible fate; and if today, society institutes a probation system, hospitalizes the mad and screens for breast cancer, when earlier it severed the hands of cabbage thieves, burnt witches at the stake and put women in scolds, this represents not an advance in human values but a change of 'calculation'. Nor can Foucault's analysis allow any final distinction to be made between the police surveillance which detains an innocent person for hours of irrelevant interrogation, and the surveillance which rescues the battered baby from its next bath of scalding water – since these are simply two instances of the same form of operation of power in the disciplining society.

Yet if there is nothing to choose between different manifestations of power in terms of their human effects (we can differentiate between them only in terms of the rationality that guides them), what ground does Foucault have for deploring the exercise of specific forms of power? Why is power resisted at all, and why some forms of it with greater vehemence than others? In the face of these difficulties, it would seem that Foucault should either have abandoned his critical political stance, or else acknowledged its reliance upon the premise of an autonomous, natural desire against which so much of his argument is explicitly directed. For since his analysis precludes any grounds for distinguishing between 'progressive' and 'regressive' dimensions of power, it is reduced to the choice between defending a 'natural' (and therefore good) desire against a (universally repressive) culture, or else reverting to the descriptivism of the structuralist account. Peter Dews has commented:

Foucault's description of the Panopticon remains a haunting evocation of the solitude and powerlessness of the individual in bourgeois society, yet his peremptory equation of subjectification and subjection erases the distinction between the enforcement of compliance with a determinate system of norms, and the formation of a reflexive consciousness which may subsequently be directed in a critical manner *against* the existing system of norms. An assessment of the modern subject, therefore, which would avoid the oscillation between irrationalist rebellion and resignation characteristic of the French philosophy of the seventies must begin by acknowledging in capitalist modernity an interplay of progressive and regressive elements far more complex than anything post-structuralism appears able to envisage.[33]

This 'oscillation' in Foucault's position renders more complex any attempted comparison of his analysis with Max Weber's critique of 'rationalization' or with the Critical Theory of the Frankfurt School.[34] If we abstract from what Foucault says about resistance, then his account of power as 'subjection' would seem to commit him to sharing Weber's belief in the inexorability of 'rationalization'; there are also similarities between the 'disciplining' practices discussed by Foucault and Weber's critique of instrumental reason and its techniques of 'rational discipline' at work.[35] On the other hand, Foucault has insisted that he is interested in specific forms of political rationality rather than in the kind of global process of rationalization theorized by Weber; and in stressing the role of human resistance to power he appears to endorse the more optimistic construction placed upon Weberian theory by the Critical Theorists and to leave open the possibility of ultimate liberation. Yet Foucault has implied that he is not a critic of capitalist rationality as such. And while the Critical Theorists have continued to link their analyses, however tenuously, to the Marxist conception of power relations as rooted in economic exploitation, and to envisage an eventual transition from capitalist alienation to a 'higher' socialist rationality, Foucault refers us only to 'anarchistic' struggles – to struggles, that is, which do not look for a 'chief' but only for an 'immediate' enemy and which 'do not expect to find a solution to their problem at a future date'.[36]

Since it implies, in fact, that a socialist rationality would simply represent a change in the calculation of political utilities, quite probably accompanied by an advance in the technologies of oppression, Foucault's analysis could seem to have only critical implications for any form of socialist project. Foucault has certainly had little to say for Marxism, dismissing it as a mere outpost of a form of nineteenth-century economic discourse of which he regards Ricardo as the true pioneer. There are none the less some grounds for attributing to Foucault an understanding of the relationship between individual action and historical process that bears direct comparison with that argued for by Marx and Engels and defended at length by Sartre in the *Critique of Dialectical Reason*. For Foucault comes close to saying in *The History of Sexuality* that the 'intentional' though 'non-subjective' quality of power relations can be viewed in 'humanist' terms as the unforeseen and unintended outcome of the mass of individual aims and objectives. Dreyfus and Rabinow stop short of imputing this conception to Foucault though they do speak of an 'historical objective' involving 'will and calculation' whose overall effect 'escapes the actors' intentions, as well as those of anybody else'; and they cite Foucault himself as saying: 'people know what they do; they frequently know why they do what they do; but what they don't know is what what they do does'.[37] Here the gap between Foucault and the phenomenologists would seem to have narrowed considerably. We might note finally that Foucault himself comes to analysing the structuralist viewpoint as an instance of 'objectivizing' knowledge. But if he does indeed regard the structuralist denial of the subject as one of the isolating, ordering and systematizing practices characteristic of disciplinary technology,[38] then ought he not to agree with the Marxists that theoretical reification of the subject is part of the problem of alienation, not its solution? In any case, it is surely an assessment that has far-reaching critical implications for Foucault's own account of 'subjectification'.

It is to the self-subverting nature of structuralist or structuralizing discourse, that Jacques Derrida has directed attention. If, as Lévi-Strauss has claimed, the structuralist theory of myths is itself mythical in status, then why, asks Derrida, have we any reason to take it seriously? He has raised a similar objection to Foucault's suggestion that his own discourse stands on a par with every other discourse: if that is so, says Derrida, how can it also be *the* discourse that reveals the equivalence of all discourses? Taking issue specifically with Foucault's account of madness, Derrida has argued that in exposing the manner in which reason silences insanity, Foucault employs a form of discourse which exemplifies those very limitations of rational thought which he wishes to reveal. *Madness and Civilisation*, for example, is scarcely a demented work; according to Foucault's central argument, therefore, it is repressing delirium in the very attempt to give it voice.[39]

Not surprisingly, Derrida has also found Foucault's work guilty of invoking an 'originary other' in its reliance upon 'madness' or the 'resistance' of an untamed bodily desire, which escapes the structurality of structure – and which is theorized as subordinated to the structure yet subversive of it. The same charge has been brought against Lévi-Strauss and Lacan – as indeed was inevitable if one considers that any theory that uses the notion of structure is bound thereby to acknowledge something which is not structure, but structured by it. Derrida's 'solution' to this dilemma is to suppress the problem: there is no fixed 'presence' of structure nor genesis of subjects, no point of origin or univocal meaning but only 'differences' and their alternation.[40]

We can look upon Derrida's 'deconstructions' of structuralist thinking as a series of *exposés* of lurking 'humanist' motifs. He himself speaks of such motifs as 'necessary' error. Yet to speak of them as mistaken in any sense is to imply that the quest for fixity of meaning is mistaken in principle (even if unavoidable in practice). The Derridian alternative to western metaphysics is the indeterminate play of 'differences', a flux wherein the dream of truth collapses in the face of an unconstrained perspectivism, and any and every meaning is equivalent to every other. In delivering all signification of a signified Derrida recasts 'truth' as randomness; and in dispensing with a subject he 'de-structures' structure, for without 'boundaries' in the subject it conditions, it ceases to retain any vestige of order or organization. In the same process, of course, he also releases the subject of any and every possible constraint. 'Structurality for Derrida', it has been said, 'it little more than a ceremonious gesture to the prestige of his immediate predecessors: its play now knows no boundaries of any sort – it is "absolute chance", "genetic indetermination", "the seminal adventure of the trace". Structure therewith capsizes into its antithesis, and post-structuralism proper is born, or what can be defined as a subjectivism, without a subject.'[41]

Notes

1 Vincent Descombes, *Modern French Philosophy*, trans. L. Scott-Fox and J. M. Harding (Cambridge 1980) p. 126.
2 ibid.
3 Louis Althusser, 'Reply to John Lewis', *Marxism Today* (October–November 1972); also Descombes, *Modern French Philosophy*, p. 169.
4 ibid., p. 168.
5 Perry Anderson, *In the Tracks of Historical Materialism* (London 1983), p. 40.
6 Ferdinand de Saussure, *Course in General Linguistics*, intro. Jonathan Culler (London 1974), 'Notes Inedites de Ferdinand de Saussure', *Cahiers Ferdinand de Saussure*, no. 12 (1954), p. 60.
6 Jacques Derrida, *Positions*, trans. Alan Bass (London 1981), pp. 15–36.
7 Saussure, *Course in General Linguistics*, p. 13 and pp. 25–9.
8 Sebastiano Timpanaro, *On Materialism* (London 1975), p. 156f.
9 ibid., p. 160.
10 'Introduction II', *Jacques Lacan and the École Freudienne, Feminine Sexuality*, ed. Juliet Mitchell and Jacqueline Rose, trans. J. Rose (London 1982), p. 42.
11 ibid., p. 118; see also p. 47.
12 Louis Althusser, *Lenin and Philosophy and Other Essays* (London 1971), p. 203.

13 ibid., pp. 213-14.
14 ibid., p. 213.
15 Giles Deleuze and Félix Guattari, *Anti-Oedipus* (London 1984); also influential was Jean-François Lyotard's *Economie Libidinale* (Paris 1974).
16 See Deleuze, *Nietzsche et la philosophie* (Paris 1962), esp. pp. 60-90.
17 Peter Dews, 'The New Philosophers', *Radical Philosophy*, no. 24 (spring 1980).
18 Bernard-Henri Lévy, *Barbarism with a Human Face*, trans. G. Holoch (New York 1979); and André Glucksmann, *The Master Thinkers*, trans. B. Pearce (New York 1980).
19 See Peter Dews, 'Power and Subjectivity in Foucault', *New Left Review*, no. 144 (March-April 1984).
20 Alan Sheridan, *Michel Foucault, the Will to Truth* (London 1980), p. 218.
21 Michel Foucault, *The Archaeology of Knowledge*, trans. A. M. Sheridan Smith (London 1972).
22 Descombes, *Modern French Philosophy*, p. 115.
23 Foucault, *The Archaeology of Knowledge*, p. 194.
24 ibid., pp. 209-10.
25 Foucault, *Discipline and Punish*, trans. Alan Sheridan (London 1979).
26 Barry Smart cites Bentham's 'Panopticon', however, as an instance of the kind of 'non-correspondence between programmes, practices and effects' in which Foucault is positively interested. See *Foucault, Marxism and Critique* (London 1983), p. 128f.
27 Foucault, 'The Subject and Power', Afterword to Hubert L. Dreyfus and Paul Rabinow, *Michel Foucault, Beyond Structuralism and Hermeneutics* (Brighton 1982), p. 211.
28 Foucault, *The History of Sexuality, Volume I: An Introduction*, trans. Robert Hurley (Harmondsworth 1980).
29 In Dreyfus and Rabinow, *Michel Foucault*, p. 221.
30 Dews, 'The New Philosophers', p. 87.
31 In Dreyfus and Rabinow, *Michel Foucault*, p. 208.
32 Smart attempts a defence in *Foucault, Marxism and Critique*, p. 104, but see also Dreyfus and Rabinow, *Michel Foucault*, p. 201f.; Dews, 'The New Philosophers', pp. 88-90.
33 Dews, ibid., p. 95.
34 By Smart, *Foucault*, pp. 123-37; see also Dews, ibid., pp. 77-86; Dreyfus and Rabinow, *Michel Foucault*, pp. 130-2, 165-7, 210;

Colin Gordon, 'Other inquisitions', *Ideology and Consciousness*, no. 6 (summer 1979).
35 See Smart, *Foucault*, pp. 130–1.
36 Foucault in Dreyfus and Rabinow, *Michel Foucault*, p. 211.
37 Dreyfus and Rabinow, ibid., pp. 187–8.
38 ibid., pp. xxii–xxiii.
39 Jacques Derrida, '*Cogito* and the History of Madness', *Writing and Difference* (Chicago 1978), pp. 31–63.
40 Derrida, *Of Grammatology* (Baltimore 1976).
41 Perry Anderson, *In the Tracks of Historical Materialism*, p. 54.

Further reading

Ferdinand de Saussure's principal work is his *Course in General Linguistics*, intro. Jonathan Culler (London 1974) (and summarized by Culler in *Saussure* (Glasgow 1976)). See also Culler's essay 'The Linguistic Basis of Structuralism', in David Robey (ed.), *Structuralism: an Introduction* (Oxford 1973). For Jacques Derrida's critique of Saussure, see the interview with Julia Kristeva in *Positions*, trans. Alan Bass (London 1981); and also *Of Grammatology*, trans. Gayatri Spivak (Baltimore 1976), which discusses speech and writing in Saussure, Lévi-Strauss and Rousseau. Jonathan Culler provides a helpful account of Derrida's reading of Saussure in *On Deconstruction: Theory and Criticism after Structuralism* (London 1983), ch. 2, i. Derrida's criticisms of Lévi-Strauss and Foucault are to be found in *Writing and Difference* (1967), trans. A. Bass (London 1978). For a short introduction to Derrida's work as a whole, see David Wood, *Radical Philosophy*, no. 21 (spring 1979).

For Jacques Lacan's writing, see *Ecrits: A Selection* (a selection from the French *Ecrits* (Paris 1966)), trans. Alan Sheridan (London 1977) – see in particular 'Agency of the letter in the Unconscious' and 'The Mirror Stage'. Anika Lemaire provides a detailed guide to Lacan's theory in *Jacques Lacan*, trans. David Macey (London 1977), while a shorter and admirably lucid account, together with critical commentary and bibliography, is to be found in David Archard, *Consciousness and the Unconscious* (London 1984). On Lacan and feminism, see *Jacques Lacan and the École Freudienne, Feminine Sexuality*, ed. Juliet Mitchell and Jacqueline Rose (London 1982); and on contemporary

French feminism in general, Elaine Marks and Isabelle de Courtrivon (eds.), *New French Feminisms* (Amherst 1980).

Few works of the 'New Philosophy' other than those by Lévy and Glucksmann are in translation, but other influential texts include: G. Lardreau and C. Jambet, 'L'Ange, entre Mao et Jesus', *Magazine Litteraire*, no. 112-13 (1976), and 'Une Derniere Fois contre la "nouvelle philosophie"', *La Nef*, no. 66 (1975); Bernard-Henri Lèvy, 'La Nouvelle Philosophie n'existe pas', *La Nef*, no. 66 (1975); M. Clavel, 'Aujourd'hui la Revolution Culturelle', *Magazine Litteraire*, no. 127-8 (1977), and P. Nemo, *L'Homme Structural* (Paris 1975). The work of Giles Deleuze and Jean-François Lyotard is discussed at some length by Vincent Descombes, *Modern French Philosophy* (London 1980); Descombes also comments briefly on the 'New Philosophy'. See also Peter Dews, 'The *Nouvelle Philosophie* and Foucault', *Economy and Society*, 8 no. 2 (1979), and 'The "New Philosophers" and the end of Leftism', *Radical Philosophy*, no. 24 (spring 1980).

Michel Foucault's key texts are: *Madness and Civilisation* (1961), trans. Richard Howard (London 1967); *Birth of the Clinic* (1963), trans. Alan Sheridan (London 1973); *The Order of Things* (1966), trans. Alan Sheridan (London 1970); *The Archaeology of Knowledge* (1969), trans. Alan Sheridan (London 1972); *Discipline and Punish* (1975), trans. Alan Sheridan (London 1977); *The History of Sexuality Vol. I: An Introduction* (1976), trans. Robert Hurley (London 1979). See also: *Language, Counter-Memory, Practice: Selected Essays and Interviews*, ed. D. F. Bouchard (Oxford 1977), and *Power/Knowledge*, ed. Colin Gordon (Brighton 1980). Sympathetic exposition of Foucault's argument is to be found in Alan Sheridan, *Michel Foucault, the Will to Truth* (London 1980); in Hubert L. Dreyfus and Paul Rabinow, *Michel Foucault, Beyond Structuralism and Hermeneutics* (Brighton 1982), in Colin Gordon, 'Birth of the Subject', *Radical Philosophy*, no. 17 (summer 1977), and in Mark Cousins, Athar Hussain, *Michel Foucault* (London 1984). Foucault's work is contrasted with that of Marx and presented as a new form of critical theory by Barry Smart, *Foucault, Marxism and Critique* (London 1983). Sharp criticism of Foucault conducted from a Marxist point of view is to be found in Perry Anderson, *In the Tracks of Historical Materialism* (London 1983); and see also Peter Dews, 'Power and Subjectivity in Foucault', *New Left Review*, no. 144 (March–April 1984).

7
The dancer or the dance? some concluding remarks

> O Body swayed to music, O brightening glance,
> How can we know the dancer from the dance?
> (W. B. Yeats)

The philosophical issues discussed in this work – the question of the relationship between human subjects and the structures in which they live; the question of the meaning and intelligibility of history; the question of alienation and of what differences exist between humanly created and natural process – all these are questions which have implications for our understanding of our political role as individuals. Indeed, the main question to which they tend – who (if anyone) makes history? – can be reformulated: in what sense, if any, is it valid for persons to conceive of themselves as conscious political agents whose decisions and actions have decisive effect on the course of history? To this question, it would seem, we have encountered three main lines of response: first, the structuralist, anti-humanist reply is that it is not valid, since the meaning of our conscious life – including our feelings of political responsibility – is inaccessible to us: we do not understand the source of our experiences nor can we learn anything helpful from them, since they are merely the surface effect of determinations exercised outside our comprehension and beyond our control.

Second, the existentialist reply is that we remain entirely responsible for what we make of our situation. We remain free agents no matter what constraints we may be under, since no factual state of the world can in anyway determine the projects of consciousness. We make of the world what we will, and our choices are fundamental.

Third, the socialist humanist reply is that people are conscious agents whose political options could be other than they are, and whose actions have real impact upon their conditions of existence. But these conditions are not themselves freely chosen. The situations in which we act have not been deliberately brought about by any individual or group, and the consequences of our actions are often themselves unforeseen and unintended. Furthermore, political agents are not necessarily aware, indeed are usually not aware, of all the factors which have conditioned their feelings and actions, even though it is not ruled out in principle that they might come to a fuller understanding of these.

To recognize persons as political agents in this third sense is not to be committed to the view that history is the progressive realization of a human essence or species-being; nor need our outlook be shaped by the 'fall and redemption' perspective invited by the theory of alienation in order for us to be able to criticize contemporary forms of existence and to advocate action to transform them. Adopting the position of Merleau-Ponty and the later Sartre, we can argue the 'openness' of history as eventuation that is neither entirely random nor wholly determined. Some of what happens is up to us even if the logic of what we do is not entirely within our grasp at any point in time.

Others have argued the more extreme case that since moral values are not rational, we remain morally responsible for our acts even if these are entirely determined. They insist, that is, that the fact that our moral values are caused in us by objective circumstances does not inform us of which of them is correct, and that judging morally and being judged are not aspects of human society that can be willed out of existence through a *theory* of determinism, even if it were correct. Kolakowski has argued that there is no logical connection between moral responsibility and the determination of human acts; that moral choices are not made easier by our being aware of them as determined; and that it would only be when we fell victim to the 'mad illusion' of having an infallible and ultimate knowledge of the laws of historical development that we could choose with facility.[1] Such a position, however, invites the objection that it evades the substantive issue of our moral freedom. Both determinist and voluntarist will agree that we experience ourselves as moral agents wracked by the torment of decision-making; the question is how far this experience of ourselves as choosing freely, and of our acts as 'decisive' *because* contingently chosen, is illusory. Does it make sense to speak of our 'responsibility' towards history if we are assuming that any exercise of 'responsibility' is itself determined by historical forces?

We might note, moreover, that the argument that individuals are the 'makers' (though not the unconditioned agents) of history is open to two rather differing constructions, which we might term respectively the 'Lukácsian' and the 'Sartrean'. According to the Lukácsian conception, the true subject of the historical process is the working class in its manifestation of an 'ascribed' consciousness – of a consciousness which its individual members would have were they in a position to assess their situation in its entirety. In speaking of 'men making history' we are therefore speaking of a collective subject – the proletariat as 'identical subject-object' – whose members are instrumental in bringing to fruition a historical project they themselves may not consciously intend. The Sartrean account, in contrast, though it emphasizes the importance of collective or class action in the making of history, maintains that in so far as a class acts as a 'subject' of history its unity is sustained only through the individual *praxes* of its members.

As we have seen, in defending this analysis, Sartre maintained that the intelligibility of history depended upon its acceptance: any known totalization must be knowable in principle to those totalized, and include a knowledge of its own structure.[2] To accept the hypothesis of a 'trans-individual' subject was to invoke a form of historical understanding inaccessible to the empirical subjects of the process, and thus to reduce Marxism to dogmatism – and determinism. 'If we do not', writes Sartre, 'wish the dialectic to become a divine law again, a metaphysical fate, it must proceed *from individuals* and not from some kind of supra-individual ensemble.'[3] In this sense, the criterion of historical understanding can never be wholly objective.

With the question of the intelligibility of history, we are brought back to a second main issue raised by the debate over humanism: that of the extent to which it is possible for humanity to be the object of its own understanding. Given that we exist within a 'cosmos' of whose origin, nature and destiny we can never have more than a very imperfect comprehension; that we are moved by emotional forces apparently prior to consciousness and unmastered by it; that the language in which we communicate, being presupposed to knowledge, appears to escape it – then in what sense can we be said to 'think' or to 'know' ourselves?

Yet the fact that our activities are not always transparent to us, should not incline us to yield without further ado to scepticism. If, for example, it is asked how we can 'think' our emotions or bodily experience, then the answer is, of course, that we cannot, and if their translation into thought is deemed essential to their knowledge, then we cannot 'know' of these aspects of our existence. Yet we may also want to claim that these are not objects of rational comprehension and that the demand for their 'knowledge' is manifesting that tendency (on which we remarked in Chapter 5) to reduce the non-cognitive to the cognitive. We may argue, that is, that such experience includes its own knowledge – a knowledge, we may add, to be elucidated further not in theory but only in art, music or literature.

Nor should we accept the suggestion that because our speech or writing depends on language for its communication, then what we say or write must be caused by something incomprehensible to us. As Saussure himself pointed out, linguistic theory confines itself to the study of the conditions of the possibility of speech-acts, and cannot hope to explain them.[4] We may argue, in any case, that the 'determination' exercised by language is of a wholly different order from that exercised by other social structures, and that the analogy with language has nothing to tell us about our capacity to comprehend and transform the latter. As Perry Anderson has put it:

Kinship cannot be compared to language as a system of symbolic communication in which women and words are respectively 'exchanged', as Lévi-Strauss would have it, since no speaker alienates vocabulary to any interlocutor, but can freely re-utilize every word 'given' as many times as is wished thereafter, whereas marriages – unlike conversations – are usually binding: wives are not recuperable by their fathers after weddings. Still less does the terminology of 'exchange' warrant an elision to the economy: if speakers and families in most societies may be reckoned to have at least a rough equivalence of words and women between them, this is notoriously not true of goods. No economy, in other words, can be primarily defined in terms of exchange at all: production and property are always prior.[5]

And he goes on to point to three more fundamental reasons why language cannot be a paradigm for social structures: its very slow rate of change; the absence of material constraint on words (which cost nothing and can be multiplied and manipulated at will); the singularity of the language-user (almost always the individual) as opposed to the plurality of the collectives (nations, classes, etc.) which are the subjects in economic, political and military matters.

But these are essentially negative arguments against the scepticism of the anti-humanists, and in pressing them we must also take note of the difficulties that Sartre's 'positive' account runs into when it comes to explaining social cohesion. If historical process is the upshot of the clash of group or class forces, themselves analysable only in terms of a convergence of the particular individuals whose will and agency sustains them, how come society does not collapse into a Hobbesian war of all against all? 'How come', as Anderson says, 'the intersection of rival collective wills does not produce the random chaos of an arbitrary, destructured log-jam?'[6] The attempt to account for the non-chaotic nature of society in terms of the integrative role of common norms and values runs up against the materialist objection that the source of any such norms or values is itself in need of explanation. Sartre was well aware of the inadequacies of such a solution to the dilemma while remaining committed to the humanist account. The problem, then, becomes that of explaining how it can be that we ascribe a meaning or 'logic' to history which is transcendent to the collectives or 'blocks of agency' involved in its creation. How, as Sartre himself put it in the unpublished second volume of the *Critique*,[7] can 'a plurality of epicentres of action have a single intelligibility' such that class struggles can be described as 'particularisations of a unitary totalization beyond them'? How, for example, can we speak of class struggle as 'contradictory'; or speculate on a logic of 'exterminism' implicit in the arms race;[8] or attribute such overall processes as 'alienation', 'rationalization', 'bureaucratization', and the like, to societies?

Discussing Sartre's attempt in the second volume of the *Critique* to provide a solution to this conundrum using as his 'raw material' the history of the USSR up to the death of Stalin, Anderson has argued that it fails in the end to offer us an account of a 'totalization without a totalizer' since Sartre is forced back upon the supposition that it was Stalin's personal power that consolidated the conflictual *praxes* of Soviet society at the time.

Hence the logic of the *Critique's* terminus in the figure of the despot himself. The effective upshot is thus paradoxically a totalization *with* a totalizer – undermining the very complexity of the historical process that it was Sartre's express purpose to establish.[9]

Anderson's own solution is to revert to the priority of the determination exercised by the mode of production. No account in terms of volition or intention, he claims, however complex or class-defined the struggle of wills, however alienated the final resultant from all of the imputed actors, can resolve the problem of social order, since this is assured prior to class struggle through the exercise of economic forces: 'the class struggle itself is not a causal prius in the sustentation of order, for *classes are constituted by modes of production and not vice-versa*'.[10]

To postulate the priority of the mode of production (or, less precisely, of the 'economic') to the clash of wills or class forces is certainly a defensible position. Yet it will not necessarily prove persuasive to the Sartrean humanist – for whom the mode of production is not shoved on to the stage of history independently of the activities of human subjects. And Marx himself acknowledges as much when he refers to the 'painful expropriation', the 'forcible methods' and the 'merciless vandalism under the stimulus of passions the most infamous' whereby the capitalist mode of production was inaugurated.[11]

It is true, none the less, that neither the mechanisms of power, nor the pain they cause, nor even the passions of those who make use of them and who are exploited by them can be analysed as unconditioned, wholly naturalistic 'inputs' into the process. If the humanist problem is to be viewed in terms of the question of the causal priority of subject or structure, then it would seem the best we can offer is a solution in terms of their interdependence. But if, in the end, we cannot improve upon the ambiguity of the conception of men and women as both 'makers' and 'made', we may also note that were the question unambiguously resoluble, it would not concern us in the first place.

Regarded from a political point of view, this indeterminacy in the relations of priority of subject and structure becomes a question of strategy: which, to put the matter crudely, is primary – the will to change (transformation of norms and values) or the change of that which conditions the will (the transformation of the material 'infrastructure')? Humanist argument tends to the assertion of the primacy of will over circumstance, anti-humanist to that of circumstance over will. But neither position taken in itself is satisfactory, and any political strategy based on appeal to the one at the expense of the other will be dangerously flawed. To take a recent contemporary example: that of the resurgence of the movement for nuclear disarmament in western Europe over the last few years. This only came about when it did because of 'circumstance': the specific sequence of developments which led to the NATO decision to deploy cruise and Pershing missiles in western Europe.

It is clearly not accountable simply to a sudden collective moral revulsion against atomic weapons. On the other hand, the conditions which the peace movement has in its turn now brought into being (where governments must consider the impact of every defence policy decision upon a public much more alert to the nuclear issue) only came into being because there existed massive numbers of rational and moral agents determined to thwart the dominant normative tendencies of their society. One can explain how this 'will to change' was generated, but what one cannot do is *to explain it away*; one cannot, that is, present it as inessential or irrelevant to the formation of the circumstances which provide the context of subsequent action and reaction.

As we have seen, it has been the tendency of the 'post-structuralist' movement to remove itself from the messy and difficult decisions of everyday politics by transposing all conflict on to the timeless and abstract plane of a struggle between the 'cultural' and the 'natural'. Instead of a conceptual framework for discriminating between different political acts and arguments, we are offerred a narrative in which hypostatized forces and entities ('desire' and 'power', 'Law' and the 'subject', 'Masters' and 'Slaves') act out their metaphorical antagonisms in extrapolation from every historical circumstance. All social eventuation, whether good or bad, is thus placed on the side of a 'culture' viewed either as necessary law or inevitable repression.

Equally incapable of discriminating between progressive and retrogressive features of our actual historical existence is the simple opposition of 'reason' and 'madness'. Indeed, those who respond to what has taken place in the name of 'Enlightenment' with a blanket condemnation of 'reason' are guilty of implicitly accepting the very conception of rationality which needs to be questioned. A much more qualified discourse is needed than that which simply opposes 'madness' to a supposedly homogeneous western 'logos' if we are to recognize or attempt to rectify the irrationalities to which Enlightenment thinking has given rise.

Similarly, if one accepts the anti-humanist cast of thought according to which affective response, whether of acceptance or rejection, is entirely constructed for subjects by the very cultural forces to which it is responding, then it becomes impossible even to question whether scientific development is conducive to human happiness; whether our needs and inclinations do simply follow upon our economic advances; whether we have the rational and moral resources to administer the effects of the technical mastery over nature now at our disposal; or whether we shall be able in the face of impending ecological and nuclear catastrophe to divert from our current path, unravel some of the history we have knitted up and 'correct' a tendency which, if it is indeed following its 'natural' course, would appear to destine our species to imminent extinction.

We must be wary, in fact, lest by focusing on the philosophical 'end of man' we encourage a passivity that may hasten the actual demise of humanity. To this suggestion, of course, it can always be objected that all efforts to control our future must themselves be viewed as part of a pre-programmed 'progression', and that we remain the mere vehicles of a determinate process even as we feel ourselves to be intervening actively to shape our species life. But such claims do nothing to undermine the importance of the distinction, central to humanist argument, between the actions we choose to take and the processes we are subject to. There are differences of degree – and of kind – between the constraints upon us to breathe, to use money, to love someone, to obey the law, to join a political party or to go on hunger strike – differences which no political or philosophical discourse can justifiably overlook.

And finally, if we wish to defend the idea that even in its most destructive acts, the human species is doing no more than fulfilling its 'natural' function, then we must also account for the profound disequilibrium it has managed to introduce into the planetary eco-system. Perhaps the annihilation of all natural life, or at least of a large part of its habitat and means of survival, that, too, is part of Nature's 'grand plan'; but if that is the case, it would seem to constitute a fairly radical rupture with its other purposes. In any case, since we must remain ignorant of any such 'design', and of our own role in it, it would seem more rational to act either as if it did not exist, or else, perhaps, to assume that our activities are destined to bring the 'Enlightenment' to that altogether more modest – and hopeful – conclusion sketched at its outset in George Herbert's poem, 'Man':

> Man is all symmetrie,
> Full of proportions, one limbe to another,
> And all to all the world besides:
> For head with foot hath private amitie
> And both with moons and tides.

Notes

1. Leszek Kolakowski, 'Conscience and Social Progress', in *Marxism and Beyond* (London 1968), pp. 151 and 156.
2. Jean-Paul Sartre, *Critique of Dialectical Reason* (London 1976), pp. 44–7; also Andre Gorz, 'Sartre and Marx', *Western Marxism, A Critical Reader* (London 1978), p. 180f.
3. ibid., p. 36.
4. Ferdinand de Saussure, *Course in General Linguistics* (London 1960), p. 13; pp. 25–9.
5. Perry Anderson, *In the Tracks of Historical Materialism* (London 1983), p. 43.
6. Perry Anderson, *Arguments within English Marxism* (London 1980), p. 51.
7. ibid., p. 52.
8. E. P. Thompson, 'Notes on Exterminism, the Last Stage of Civilisation', *New Left Review*, no. 121 (1980) (see also E. P. Thompson and others, *Exterminism and Cold War*, (London 1982)).
9. Perry Anderson, *Arguments*, p. 53.
10. Louis Althusser, *For Marx* (London 1966), pp. 117–28.
11. Karl Marx, *Capital*, vol. I (London 1974) p. 714.

Index

Aquinas, Thomas 14
Adorno, Theodor 22, 78
Algiers 122
alienation 29-32, 49, 58, 64-5, 68-9, 72-4, 84, 87-8, 99-100, 102-4, 115-16, 146-7, 150
Althusser, Louis 10, 12, 50, 88-90, 93-4, 96-9, 113-18, 120, 128-9, 142, 154; *works*: *Elements of Self-Criticism* (1974) 107, 116-17; *For Marx* (1966) 93, 99-103, 112, 116-17, 154; *Lenin and Philosophy and other Essays* (1964-70) 99, 116-17, 142; *Reading Capital* (1968) 99, 102, 106-10, 117
Anderson, Perry 86, 92-3, 95, 113, 116-17, 142, 144, 145, 149, 154
anthropocentricism 24-6, 46-7
Archard, David 50, 78, 144
Aristotle 22
Aron, Raymond 81
Aronson, Ronald 73, 76-8, 91
Arthur, Chris 49-52
Austin, John 108, 117
Avineri, Shlomo 52
Axelos, Kostas 84, 95
Ayer, Alfred J. 13, 22, 108

Bacon, Francis 15
Bahro, Rudolf 42, 50
Balibar, Etienne 105, 106; *works*: *see* Althusser (*Reading Capital*)

Bannan, John 78
de Beauvoir, Simone 62-4, 75, 77, 91, 94-5; *works*: *The Second Sex* (1949) 62-4, 75, 77
Bentham, Jeremy 137, 143
Benton, Ted 118
Bergson, Henri 44, 52
Berkeley, Bishop 108
Bhaskar, Roy 119
Biemel, Walter 77
Blackburn, Robin 49
Bouchard, D. F. 145
'British Althusserianism' 110-12
British Humanist Association 9, 13, 15, 17
Bukharin, Nikolai 80, 83, 90
Burnier, M. A. 91

Calvez, J. Y. 88, 92
Campana, Augusto 22
capitalism 15-16, 40-2, 69, 79, 104, 130-1
Cartesianism *see* Descartes
Castoriadis, Cornelius 75, 84-5, 91-2
catholicism 88, 92
Caute, David 95
China 87-8, 113
Chiodi, Pietro 78
Clarke, Simon 118
Clavel, Maurice 131, 145
Colletti, Lucio 118
Collier, Andrew 118

INDEX

Collins, M.   75
Communist Party of China   87, 92
Communist Party of Great Britain   93
Communist Party of the Soviet Union   80
Cornu, Auguste   88, 92
de Courtrivon, Isabelle   145
Cousineau, Robert   77
Cousins, Mark   145
Croce, Benedetto   50
Culler, Jonathan   142, 144
Cultural Revolution (Chinese)   88
Czechoslovakia   85

Deleuze, Giles   122, 130-1, 143, 145
Della Volpe, Galvano   45
Derrida, Jacques   11, 17, 23, 77, 96-7, 120, 122, 124, 141-2, 144
Descartes, René   14, 55, 64, 98, 101-2
Descombes, Vincent   50, 142, 143, 145
Dews, Peter   131, 139, 143, 145
dialectic   25-30, 45-6, 68-78, 131, 148-50
Dickens, Charles   23
Dilthey, W.   44
le Doeuff, Michelle   77
Dreyfus, Hubert L.   140, 143, 145
Duclos, Jacques   83
Dunayevskaya, Raya   92-3
Duvigneaud, Jean   84

Einstein, Alfred   55
Engels, Friedrich   31, 40, 43, 49, 52, 68, 76, 80, 84, 140; *works*: *see* Marx (*The German Ideology*)
Enlightenment   12-16, 120, 132, 152
Epicureanism   16
Erasmus   22
Eurocommunism   89-90
existentialism   16, 18, 47-8, 52-3, 59-64, 79, 89, 134, 146

experience   55-6, 66-7, 79, 114-15, 148-9; *see also* phenomenology
Eysenck, H. J.   14

Fay, Brian   119
feminism   62-4, 127-30
Feuerbach, Ludwig   24, 31-5, 40-1, 49, 51-2, 100-1, 112
Fichte, Johann   26-8, 46, 49
'Frankfurt School'   52-3, 92, 139
Freud, Sigmund   14, 111, 122, 125, 128, 130
Freudianism *see* Freud; Lacan; psychoanalysis
Fromm, Erich   92
Foucault, Michel   10, 12, 17, 88, 89, 92, 96-7, 116, 120, 122, 132-45; *works*: *The Archaeology of Knowledge* (1969)   89, 133; *Discipline and Punish* (1975) 136-7
Fougeyrollas, Pierre   84, 95

Garaudy, Roger   45, 49-50, 52, 88, 94
Geras, Norman   49, 118
Giddens, Anthony   119
Glucksmann, André   92, 95, 118, 131
Goldmann, Lucien   43, 50, 75, 84
Gordon, Colin   144, 145
Gorz, Andre   73-6, 78, 154
Gould, C.   75
Gramsci, Antonio   42, 45, 50, 52
Guattari, Felix   130, 143, 145

Habermas, Jürgen   119
Hall, Stuart   86, 93-4
Hegedus, A.   95
Hegel, G. W. F.   18, 23-4, 26, 28-32, 34-6, 41, 43, 45-54, 57, 63, 66, 85, 80; *works*: *Phenomenology of Spirit* (1807)   31, 46-7, 49, 51-2
Heidegger, Martin   10, 18, 23-4,

INDEX

56–61, 75–7, 84; *works: Being and Time* (1926) 59, 76; 'Letter on Humanism' (1947) 58–60, 75–7
Held, David 53, 78
Herbert, George 153
Hindess, Barry 118
Hirsh, A. 91, 94–5
Hirst, Paul 110–12, 117
history, historicism 19–21, 72–4, 98–9
Hobbes, Thomas 101–2
Horkheimer, Max 22
Hulme, T. E. 21
Hume, David 26
Hungary 83–5
Hunt, Alan 94
Hussain, Athar 145
Husserl, Edmund 18, 23–5, 45, 55, 60, 66, 75–7
Hyppolite, Jean 47, 51–2

idealism 24–30, 35–40, 46–7
Indonesia 87
industrialization, critique of 15–16, 41–5, 152–3

Jambet, C. 131, 145
James, William 14
Jay, Martin 53, 78

Kant, Immanuel 14, 24, 26–8, 55–6, 68
Kantianism *see* Kant
Kaufman McCall, D. 77
Kautsky, K. 80, 90
Keat, Russell 119
Khrushchev, Nikita 85, 87
Kierkegaard, Sören 43, 47–8, 53
Kojève, Alexandre 45–7, 50–1, 54, 66; *works: Introduction to the Reading of Hegel* (1947) 45–52
Kolakowski, Leszek 49, 52, 92, 118, 147, 154

Korsch, Karl 43, 45, 52, 85
Kosik, Karel 86, 92
Kristeva, Julia 144
Kruks, Sonia 77, 91
Kurst, Paul 22

Labedz, Leopold 93
Labica, Georges 52
Lacan, Jacques 96–7, 115, 120, 122, 125–30, 137, 141, 144–5
Lardreau, G. 131, 145
Larrain, Jorge 118
Lefebvre, Henri 52, 84, 95
Lefort, Claude 84–5
Lenin, V. I. 87
Lévi-Strauss, Claude 10, 12, 89, 97–9, 116–17, 127, 141, 144, 149
Lévy, Bernard-Henri 92, 131–2
linguistics *see* de Saussure
Lloyd, Genevieve 63, 75, 77
Locke, John 14, 52
Lowrie, Walter 53
Lukács, Georg 23, 42–5, 54, 58, 75–6, 84–5, 89, 148; *works: History and Class Consciousness* (1923) 43–5, 52
Lyotard, Jean-François 143, 145

McClellan, David 52, 92
Mallin, S. B. 78
Maoism 87–8
Marcuse, Herbert 52, 78
Markovic, Mihailo 86, 92, 95
Marks, Elaine 145
Marx, Karl 12, 20–2, 24–5, 31–45, 49–54, 64–5, 68–70, 76, 78, 80, 83–119, 120–2, 130–2, 138, 140, 145; *works: Capital* (1867) 50, 100, 102–5, 116, 54; *Contribution to Hegel's Philosophy of Law. Introduction* (1843) 33, 51;

157

INDEX

Marx, Karl – cont.
  Economic and Philosophic
  Manuscripts of 1844   32–7,
  49, 52, 84–5, 87–8, 92; *The*
  German Ideology (1845–6)   38–40, 43,
  49–50, 52–3, 68–9, 112, 115
Marxism *see* Engels; Marx; socialism
Master–Slave dialectic   29–30, 47, 51,
  62–4, 152
May 1968   85, 88–90, 94–5, 121,
  130–3
Mepham, John   78, 106–7, 116–18
Meredith, George   23
Merleau-Ponty, Maurice   47–8, 64–7,
  75–8, 81–3, 91, 147; *works: Adventures*
  of the Dialectic (1955)   78, 82;
  Humanism and Terror (1947)   78, 91;
  Phenomenology of Perception
  (1945)   77–8; *Sense and Non-Sense*
  (1948)   64–5, 75, 77
Meszaros, Istvan   77–8
Mill, John Stuart   80
Miller, A. V.   51
Mitchell, Juliet   142, 144
moralism, morality   113–16, 118–19,
  147–8
More, Thomas   22
Morin, Edgar   84
Morris, William   76

Nairn, Tom   93
NATO   79, 151
Neo-Hegelians   43
'New Philosophers'   130–2
Nietzsche, Friedrich   12, 17, 88, 92,
  122, 130, 133

objectification *see* alienation
Ollivier, Albert   81
O'Neill, John   52
Owen, Robert   23

Parti Communiste Française (PCF)   80–4,
  88–90
Patton, Paul   94
Pearson, Gabriel   93
Petrovic, Gaia   86, 92, 95
Petty, William   101
phenomenology   16–18, 29, 45–6,
  54–60, 70
'philosophy of desire'   130–2
Pico della Mirandola   22
Pierce, C.   75
Plato   22
Plekhanov, Georg   80, 91
Poland   85, 92
positivism   13–14, 44, 54, 58, 60, 70,
  138
Poster, Mark   78
post-structuralism *see* structuralism
Poulantzas, Nicos   89–90
praxis   36, 45, 68–71, 76, 84, 148, 150
Praxis group   86, 92
Proudhon, Pierre   39
Proudhonian socialists   41
psychoanalysis   67, 111, 125–30; *see*
  also Freud; Lacan

Rabinow, P.   140, 143, 145
Rancière, Jacques   118
Rassemblement Democratique
  Revolutionaire   82, 91
Read, Herbert   21
Rée, Jonathan   76–7, 93–4
Renaissance   14–15, 21–2
Ricardians   41
Ricardo, David   101, 140
Robey, David   78, 144
Rosandra, Rosanna   96
Rose, Jacqueline   142, 144
Rosenthal, G.   91
Rousseau, Jean Jacques   27, 79,
  101–2, 144
Rousset, D.   91

158

INDEX

Rubel, M. 88, 92
Ruben, David Hillel 118
Russia *see* USSR
Ryazanov, David 92

Samuel, R. 93
Sartre, Jean-Paul 18, 23, 25, 47-8, 59-77, 80-4, 89, 91, 95, 98, 116, 140, 147-8, 150, 154; *works*: *Being and Nothingness* (1943) 60-2, 64, 66-8, 81; *Critique of Dialectical Reason* (1960) 68-74, 76-7, 98, 107, 140, 150, 154; *What is Literature?* (1948) 68-9, 77
de Saussure, Ferdinand 16-17, 97, 123-6, 142, 144, 154
Saville, John 86
Sayer, Derek 118
Schelling, F. W. J. von 24, 28, 46
Schmidt, Alfred 53
Sheridan, Alan 133, 143, 144, 145
Sino-Soviet conflict 87-8
Skillen, Tony 118
Skinner, B. F. 13
Smart, Barry 143, 145
socialism 32-3, 40-2, 72-4, 84-7, 93, 130-2
socialist humanism 85-7, 92-4, 112-15, 146
Solzhenitsyn, A. 131
Soviet Union *see* USSR

Stalin, Joseph 72, 80, 83-8, 91, 95, 113, 131-2, 150
Stalinism *see* Stalin; socialist humanism
Stedman Jones, Gareth 23, 44, 50
structuralism, post-structuralism 16-18, 88-90, 96-9, 120-5, 132-3, 137-42, 146, 149-53
subject–object identity *see* dialectic, Lukács

Taylor, Charles 93
Third World 74, 87
Thompson, E. P. 23, 76, 86, 93-4, 108-11, 117-18, 154
Timpanaro, Sebastiano 118, 142
Trotsky, Leon 84

USA 81-2, 87
USSR 81-2, 84-7, 113, 150

Vico, G. 76

Warsaw Pact 79
Wartofsky, M. 75
Waterhouse, Roger 77
Weber, Max 44, 139, 140
Williams, Raymond 21
Wittgenstein, Ludwig 17
Wundt, W. 14

Yang, Chou 87
Yugoslavia 85